THE ART OF CREAT

Recent research has repeatedly confirmed that it is not the technique nor the theory, but the interaction between therapists and clients that creates change in clients. This practical guide outlines the ways in which psychotherapists can find new methods of moving their therapy sessions toward dynamic, healing interactions by shifting away from an overreliance on techniques and theories.

The Art of Creating a Magical Session discusses the key elements needed to create the interaction conditions for transformational therapeutic change to occur. Using a conceptual approach to client transformation, the book draws from a diverse range of sources including indigenous traditions and rituals, as well as the latest research on the common factors that contribute to success in the therapy room. Each chapter focuses on educating and inspiring mental health professionals to easily adapt and apply creative and resourceful approaches to help their own clients begin inner transformations.

With case studies and narratives woven throughout, this accessible guide will support mental health practitioners as they approach their practice in new ways and achieve deeper, and more magical, therapy sessions. It will be valuable reading for psychotherapists, psychologists, social workers, and counselors.

Paul J. Leslie, EdD, is a psychotherapist, researcher, trainer, and author in Aiken, South Carolina. He specializes in resource directed approaches to working with individuals and families. Paul is a licensed professional counselor in the states of Georgia and South Carolina, and a National Board certified Fellow in Hypnotherapy. He has a doctorate in Counseling Psychology and is presently the coordinator of the psychology program at Aiken Technical College, SC.

THE ART OF CREATING A MAGICAL SESSION

Key Elements for Transformative Psychotherapy

Paul J. Leslie

Routledge
Taylor & Francis Group

NEW YORK AND LONDON

First published 2019
by Routledge
52 Vanderbilt Avenue, New York, NY 10017

and by Routledge
2 Park Square, Milton Park, Abingdon, Oxon, OX14 4RN

Routledge is an imprint of the Taylor & Francis Group, an informa business

Library of Congress Cataloging-in-Publication Data
Names: Leslie, Paul J., author.
Title: The art of creating a magical session: key elements for transformative psychotherapy / Paul J. Leslie.
Description: New York, NY: Routledge, 2019. | Includes bibliographical references and index.
Identifiers: LCCN 2018040528 (print) | LCCN 2018041129 (ebook) | ISBN 9780429430640 (E-book) | ISBN 9781138365629 (hardback) | ISBN 9781138365636 (pbk.) | ISBN 9780429430640 (ebk) Subjects: | MESH: Psychotherapy-methods
Classification: LCC RC480.5 (ebook) | LCC RC480.5 (print) | NLM WM 420 | DDC 616.89/14–dc23
LC record available at https://lccn.loc.gov/2018040528

ISBN: 9781138365629 (hbk)
ISBN: 9781138365636 (pbk)
ISBN: 9780429430640 (ebk)

Typeset in ITC Legacy Serif
by Deanta Global Publishing Services, Chennai, India

T O ALL WHO WALK THE PATH OF THE HEALER

CONTENTS

FOREWORD

I had the privilege of spending time with Milton Erickson, MD, toward the end of his life, and was enchanted by his flexibility, humanity, and dedication to helping people realize more of the resources that they had, were unaware of, or had forgotten. He told me that he had a phone call from a woman who had been washing her hands obsessively for 12 years. Erickson was very interested to know what she did with her hands 13 years ago, not the nature or cause of her problem or treating a condition. He was focusing instead on what might be helpful to create a solution, one unique to her.

Erickson's emphasis on honoring the uniqueness of every client and tailoring his approach to each individual was revolutionary, and while there is a growing appreciation of these principles, there remains a persistent fashion to find a single approach for all people and then apply it. Conservative forces can be very strong and very appealing.

In my view, Erickson was a healer. He was interested in a holistic approach before the word existed, and he encouraged others to look at the big picture and not be limited by some hypothetical theory. His invitation to develop our peripheral vision may have been practical, and also metaphoric.

Erickson was interested in anthropology and shamanic practices, and although he never mentioned 'magic,' much of his work and teaching were experienced as being 'magical.' Many people read about his cases and are stunned by the miracles that occurred. It is tempting to think of him as a magician. He said that all he ever did was to practice simple, commonsense psychology, and, that in itself, may have been the source of the magic that we see.

Over the last 40 years, I have continued to be inspired by what I learned with that maverick and I have applied it to my clinical work and teaching with ongoing joy and satisfaction.

Erickson encouraged clients and practitioners to develop interests outside of their work, so our perspective could be widened and more flexible. After my time with him, I have discovered wonderful contributions to my therapy learning coming from disparate sources: Humberto Maturana as a biologist, Heinz von Foerster as a curiologist, Lao Tzu's timeless Tao Te Ching, Zen writings, personal development gurus like Werner Erhard and Bob Hoffman, and more recently, Paul Leslie's contributions about magic ... the list goes on ... all have been 'outside the square' of the field of psychotherapy. I continue to appreciate foreign, even alien, cultures as opportunities to shed light on my blind spots and loosen rigidities, known or unknown.

I first met Dr. Paul Leslie at an Ericksonian conference a few years ago in an eye-opening workshop he presented about Conjure – the magical and healing practices of the Coastal Carolinas and Georgia. I then read his fascinating book, 'Low Country Shamanism,' about these practices where 'Root doctors' performed rituals and healed people. I was fascinated. From our first meeting, it was obvious to me that Paul's innovative approach added substance and breadth to hypnosis and therapy, and one which resonated with me because of his genuine humility, creativity, and flexibility.

Paul's invitation to bring magic back into therapy can seem to come from left field at first, but it is appealing and timely since too much psychotherapy has devolved into a mechanistic, inhuman application of some rigid theory or protocol, which, at best will only help a few, and at worst, will create stuckness and resistance. He recurrently and convincingly shows that magic – although, or perhaps because, it is 'outside the square' of the field of psychotherapy – can add to the breadth and depth of what we therapists can offer our clients.

In this book, between the Introduction and Epilogue, Paul offers seven chapters where he outlines the principles of bringing magic into a session, the unknown, the alliance, experiences, frames, nonlinear thinking, and rituals – all pivotal areas for creating change and healing.

Any therapist who is serious about their work will naturally be interested to explore them.

In each chapter, he outlines the ways that magic can contribute, extensively quotes other experts to add texture and solidness, and illustrates with cases from his own practice. The result is a charming, inviting exploration of the benefits of including magic in psychotherapy.

Paul Leslie's genuineness and creativity permeate the whole book and readers of all persuasions, and all levels of experience, will learn about the benefits to the client and therapist of including magic, and even more importantly, they will be able to know the practicalities of how to do this. I did, and I recommend this important book wholeheartedly.

Dr. Rob McNeilly
Co-director, The Milton H Erickson Institute of Tasmania

ACKNOWLEDGMENTS

There are so many wonderful people to acknowledge. I want to particularly recognize the following mentors, colleagues, and friends:

Dana Rideout, Bette Freedson, Richard Hill, Susan Davis, Rob McNeilly, Gabrielle Peacock, Scott Miller, Bob Bertolino, Elliot Connie, Bill O'Hanlon, Lisa Dion, Shelly Allman, Thomas Abernathy, Mike Munion, Steve Hoskinson, Eric Greenleaf, Suzanne Black, Stephen Brooks, Robert Musikantow, Courtney Armstrong, Rick Miller, and Tara Dickherber.

Thank you to Clare Ashworth at Routledge whose attention, helpfulness, and professionalism made the process of creating this book a gratifying one.

My sincere appreciation goes out to my clients whose courage and resilience continues to fill me with amazement, admiration, and gratitude.

Most importantly, I remain thankful to my parents, Paul and Sue Leslie, who have always been my greatest supporters.

INTRODUCTION

For most of my professional career as a psychotherapist, I have been perplexed about what it is that makes the difference between an 'effective' therapy session and a 'transformational' therapy session. An effective session is one in which the goals of treatment have been met. A transformational session is one in which, not only have treatment goals been met, but a radical shift has also taken place in how clients view themselves and their situations. I found it was fairly easy to measure treatment goal attainment, but I found it was a much more difficult attempting to measure transformation.

Having an effective session should always be a goal for us as practitioners. However, we all know that our sessions can be more than just facilitating a decrease in clients' presenting symptoms. Having clients lower their anxiety is a desirable outcome, but lowering their anxiety while also having an amazing life-changing moment is something completely different.

My first therapy job was in a nonprofit community mental health agency in a rural area. I had the good fortune of working with a wide variety of cases with people from various socio-economic and racial backgrounds. The work was challenging and it strengthened my confidence in my therapeutic abilities. I also made quite a few mistakes along the way which also taught me many valuable lessons of what not to do.

During that time, I began the practice of charting how each of my sessions had gone. I listed the theme of the session and what interventions I had used. In doing this, I became more aware of what worked for

1

me and what didn't work. At that time, I believed that if I had a transformative session it was because I had employed a specific therapy technique at the right time in the session which created change. I thought that if I could find a pattern in my work that had been successful, I could then replicate this pattern in all of my other sessions for similar successes.

The search for a pattern that would give me unlimited success in my work failed to materialize. Yes, there were some techniques that appeared to work often, but I could find no pattern for knowing when, where, and how to use the techniques that would give me certainty in success. After realizing that the charting of sessions was not fruitful, I then began to change my theoretical orientation. I assumed that it must be the theory being used that stood in the way of my success. After utilizing several theories for a few years, and finding the same results, I had to accept that perhaps there was something beyond the use of technique and theory that created transformational outcomes in therapy.

When my quest for the perfect technique and theory did not pan out, I began to explore whether there were similarities between psychotherapy and other healing traditions. I was curious how people experienced transformation outside of a therapy room. I found that I had to set aside the preconceptions of my therapy training and become open to other concepts, concepts that were often outside my comfort zone.

During this quest, I interviewed a variety of healers ranging from Indian Swamis to Tibetan monks, bodyworkers, psychics, neurobiologists, and shamans. It was an eye-opening experience for me because many things that I heard challenged my belief system. In spite of the wide variety of opinions on how to create healing transformations, eventually, several concepts emerged which were consistent with the work I performed as a psychotherapist.

In my journey to discover these similarities between psychotherapy and other approaches to healing, I spent some time exploring an indigenous tradition located in my own geographic region, the magical and healing traditions of the Gullah. The Gullah are the descendants of African slaves who, after the Civil War, lived in the isolated coastal plain and Sea Islands area of the United States. They developed their own language and culture that was opulent in African influences. In the ethnographic exploration of the Gullah, I discovered a unique system of healing based on oral tradition and ancestral transmission, which they called 'hoodoo' or 'conjure.' It was a fascinating excursion into a system which has its roots in ancient spiritual practices that span several millennia.

The practitioners of hoodoo are often called 'root doctors' because of their traditional use of plant roots to treat physical and psychological ailments. The root doctors make magical potions designed to bring their clients everything from good health to money or even love. The roots may also be used for less sanguine results since it is not uncommon in the area to hear of someone 'getting the root put on them.' This means a spell has been fixed onto an individual by a root doctor; however, most of the root doctors I encountered were only interested in performing healing and spiritual work.

It was a conversation with one of the root doctors that made the entire concept of a magical therapy session click for me. In our discussion about healing practices, one practitioner told me that he believed that the root doctor was not really directly responsible for the magic which took place, but rather, the root doctor created the 'conditions' for the magic to occur. He said that people came to him for a variety of reasons, but they all wanted his help in changing their situations. He said that all he could do was to set up conditions so that the magic could manifest. He firmly believed that the people who came to see him were just as important in creating change as the root doctor in the practice of hoodoo. He felt that root doctors could do little magic or healing if there was not an environment of openness and connection between root doctors and their clients.

Reflecting on our conversation, I had an epiphany. His comments were not unlike those of the other healing practitioners with whom I had spoken. Although though they were from radically different backgrounds, these healers believed that transformation only took place if certain conditions were in place and if the person needing the transformation was open to change. This gave me a new perspective about my own work as a therapist. If a psychotherapist is not directly responsible for the transformation of their clients, then the therapist's primary job is to create the conditions for change to occur. It is not the specific technique or theory being used, but rather it is the formulation of the interaction which brings forth transformation.

I set about studying everything I could about interaction in the therapy room and what ingredients of a therapy session could create the conditions for change to occur. In my own work as a therapist, I became less interested in rigidly applying any theory or technique. Instead, I began to see therapy as a spontaneous interaction in which anything could occur, and that the experience of therapy could become magical and transformative if a lively, synergetic quality existed between the client and the therapist. However, there also needed to be an element of surprise and novelty which could cause unexpected shifts away from the clients' rigid patterns of thinking, emotion, and behavior. I now understood why some practitioners view therapy as 'interactive performance with the therapist improvising in response to, or in dance with, the client' (Gibney, 2012, p. 67).

With this new approach to doing therapy, I found that magical sessions can occur with most of the client population. Fortunately, at the time I was working at a practice that saw people from all walks of life, from a wide variety of socio-economic and ethnic backgrounds. I worked with clients who were experiencing minor life change issues, while others had been labeled seriously mentally ill. I found that when I let go of preconceptions of how a session should proceed and instead just jumped into the moment, many magical events would take place. If I did my best to create the conditions for magical transformation in the session, transformation would often take place.

Thus, I began my moving away from the way I had normally done sessions in the past, which focused on replicating the techniques and theories of other therapists. Instead, there was a new openness to using whatever was helpful and ethical in helping my clients. Letting go of familiar patterns of interventions gave new energy and creativity to my work. I still used the skills I had honed over many years, but there was now a freedom to use them in a more flexible manner.

The therapy room became a place to discover the strengths and resources within clients themselves, who often did not believe they had any. Imaginative experiences were constructed on the spot depending on the needs of the specific client. I had clients to whom I sang to, with whom I danced with, those I teased and provoked, others were soothed, some were argued with, and others cried with in the effort to create a session where magical transformation could occur. I am now certain that great therapy is indeed more about having a powerful connection and interaction between client and therapist, than about any specific intervention or theory.

Memorable cases that became magical included a father and son who had been estranged for years finally making an emotional connection when they were instructed to talk to each other as if they were professional wrestlers. A woman was finally able to let go of her painful past when all the furniture in the therapy room had been turned upside down. A mother who saw herself as a doormat made significant changes after a large rug was thrown onto her lap. A self-professed kleptomaniac changed her behavior after being given permission and free rein to steal anything in the therapy office. A client experienced a tremendous shift in how she viewed herself after a poem had been read to her.

For a therapy session to be really transformative, a large dose of creativity on the part of the therapist is usually needed. As Miller (in Kotter & Carlson, 2009) wisely put it, 'Creativity means utilizing clients' resources and abilities in a way that leads them beyond whatever's obstructing their path onto a more creative life' (p. 115). We have to bravely relinquish our pre-established ideas and applications about what should happen in a session and, instead, open up to the unexplored territory that exists between clients and therapists. This can yield magical moments.

Some therapists may be apprehensive about introducing more creativity in their work. Because of unwarranted fears, countless professionals in the psychotherapeutic arena often discourage themselves from paying attention to the inner wisdom that they possess. If trained and seasoned therapists are following all ethical guidelines, there is no reason not to invite more creativity into their work. It is creativity that gives our sessions life. As Neimeyer (in Kotter & Carlson, 2009) stated, 'Every psychotherapy session is an invitation to creativity. When we decline this invitation, we deaden ourselves as therapists and we deaden our clients as people who consult us' (p. 159).

Too often, many well-intentioned therapists may actually move their clients away from the potential of having a magical experience. These therapists usually have been trained to believe that therapy should follow a very strict protocol and that clients must adhere to the protocol. Unfortunately, confining interaction does nothing to bring forth transformation. Please understand, I do not advocate that therapists throw away all their best tools. I am merely encouraging therapists to consider that their already effective tools could be even more transformational in an environment of fascination and enchantment.

The result of my journey is the book you are now reading. I am sharing the ideas with you that I have found to be necessary in creating the conditions for a magical session. I have included many case stories to illustrate the concepts that this work will cover (the names and identifying information of clients have been changed to protect privacy). My hope is that whatever your theoretical orientation, you will find a spark inside you that nudges you to move beyond just being an 'effective' therapist. I truly believe that we, as psychotherapists, can do even more for our clients than just alleviate symptoms. We can assist them in ways that can only be called 'magical.'

CHAPTER 1

WHAT IS A MAGICAL SESSION?

The term 'magic' conjures up different images for people. Some may instantly think of the exciting illusionists' stage shows where misdirection and sleight of hand thrill and delight audiences. Others may think of the fantasy tales of wizards and dragons that capture the imagination and provide readers with hours of escapist enjoyment. While others may think of occult practices where practitioners perform elaborate ceremonies to create mystical experiences.

The one factor that all these images of magic have in common is that there is a departure from the normality of everyday life. Having a 'magical' experience is out of the realm of the ordinary and allows a peek behind the veil of the mysterious. These experiences can be profound and even possibly life changing for individuals who are open to allowing this magic into their awareness.

It is the assertion of this book that for psychotherapy to be truly transforming, the therapeutic practitioner must make therapy sessions a 'magical' experience. To understand how the term, magical, will be used throughout this book, we turn to a definition found in the English Oxford Dictionary ('Magical,' 2018):

Magical [maj-i-kuh l]: *'beautiful and delightful in such a way as to seem removed from everyday life'*

This definition sums up what therapists should aim to be for a client's experience. I specifically want to emphasize being 'removed from everyday life.' It is crucial for our clients that they have an experience in their therapy session that is radically different from what they usually encounter in their daily living. Defining what a magical experience is can be difficult due to the limitations of our descriptive language, but it is embodied in the sense of wonder that something, somehow, has changed from the standard and the familiar into something that is enchanted and profound. It is beyond words or logical explanations.

I view magic in therapy as a metaphorical exploration for bringing forth the innate ingenuity that resides in both client and therapist. Working from this perspective, we value connection and inspiration over predictability and pathology. By opening a space for creativity and surprise, we set the conditions for magic to occur in our therapy sessions. A magical session is different with each client, each session, and each therapist. The loss of a magical session occurs when the therapist is locked into the use of rigid, habitual methods for conceptualizing cases combined with an excessive and unrelenting focus on client deficits.

I am not the first clinician to advocate for psychotherapy to be a magical experience (and I hope that I am not the last). I believe that the more magical a session can be, the more transforming it can be. A magical session encourages therapists to create out of the ordinary therapy applications that surprise both the clients and themselves. In this context of the extraordinary, we find ourselves taking actions and sharing ideas as we have never previously done. We move away from the safe and familiar. We move into the realm of the unknown. We find new, inventive, and unique ways to approach cases that are so out of character for us that we may wonder from where our ideas came.

Instead of structured, lifeless treatment methods, a magical session is a dynamic and energetic interaction in which spontaneity and creative action abound. Each therapeutic encounter is a unique experience that is co-created by all parties involved. It summons the presence of possibility, hope, and imagination. It pushes a therapist to move beyond the comfort of their training and to become open to what may occur in the present moment. A magical session includes a space for the unknown with freedom to explore the unfamiliar and to allow our creative genius to roam. I remember reading that William James, known as the Father of American Psychology, believed that a genius was really just someone who had an ability to perceive things in a non-habitual way.

Working in the field of psychotherapy is often routine. We find ourselves dealing with the same problems, using the same techniques, and perhaps even telling the same stories and using the same metaphors. When our goal is to have a magical session, we must move out of familiar patterns for performing therapy. When making the creation of a magical interaction with our clients a priority, we find that our useful clinical skills and techniques become supercharged, and we move effortlessly to facilitate changes and transformation in the lives of our clients.

In many hours spent watching videos and reading transcripts of the many great therapists in our field, I have come to the conclusion that these therapy giants weren't effective only because they had the best theory or technique. They were great therapists because they created an out of the ordinary environment for their clients. Their active engagement with their clients are what set the conditions for their theories to spring to life. Unfortunately, our sterile mimicry of these giants' theories appears only as hollow caricatures of truly dynamic therapy and magical engagement. The adventurous spirit of the many brilliant minds that helped to create and to develop the field of psychotherapy has taken a backseat to the new focus on regimentation and specialization, reductionist pharmacological processes, and high-cost certification programs that promise to be the missing link in eradicating client pathology.

We often forget that when people today seek help from a therapist, they are doing what our ancestors did when they turned to shamans, wisdom keepers, and prophets for thousands of years. The hope was, and still is, that someone will aid them in alleviating their emotional pain. Seeking relief from their pain has pushed many to look beyond the advice of friends and family members, and seek out someone who is wise and experienced in the art of 'healing.' As Yeh, Hunter, Madan-Bahal, Chiang, and Arora (2004) state:

> For centuries, healers have been recognized as individuals who are acknowledged in their communities as possessing special insight and helping skills. These individuals are commonly recognized as healers and are believed to possess special skills that grow out of timeless wisdom. Healers are keepers of this wisdom and enlist it to help people solve problems and make decisions.
>
> *(p. 411)*

9

Psychotherapy vs. Healing

Take a moment to ask yourself why did you become a therapist? Allow your mind to fully examine all the reasons that made you want to take the plunge into the world of psychotherapy. Be as clear and as honest with yourself as possible. Examine any motivation or experience that nudged you into entering the 'helping profession.' Capture all the 'whys' that propelled you through years of graduate school, internships, and direct practice.

If you are like the countless people whom I questioned over the last few years, you probably answered in one of three answers: (1) to help others; (2) to make the world a better place; or (3) to help myself heal (to paraphrase Erich Fromm, many therapists keep waiting to meet the client that will help them heal). No one has ever replied that they want to make more money or for celebrity status. It appears that the desire to heal motivates most of us as we enter a profession that generally often offers long hours, low pay, and is emotionally taxing.

Now, pause again and ask yourself how you envisioned a healing psychotherapy session before you became a therapist. Did you envision yourself being emotionally distant while sitting with someone in emotional distress? Did you envision yourself constantly scribbling notes down on a clipboard? Did you envision standardized treatment plans? Did you envision yourself giving a monotone delivery of the latest therapy homework assignment to your client?

I am guessing that your response to all those questions is 'no.' Most of us did not envision what we have grown to accept as 'proper' psychotherapy today. The emphasis on treatment planning, insurance billing, swift diagnosing, and the strict guidelines of 'evidence-based' therapies has replaced much energy and creativity in the therapy room. As one of my colleagues recently told me, 'these days the way most therapy is performed is just plain dull.'

I can remember my early days as a new therapist working in a community mental health center. I was inspired to help people change their lives for the better. I voraciously read everything I could find about every form of psychotherapy. I attended training that I hoped would teach me how to create magical outcomes in my therapy work. Over time, though, I lost the passion for what I did. Many of the approaches I had been taught were devoid of inspiration or positive connotation. The more I learned about 'therapy,' the more I began to abandon my enthusiasm and creativity, and the more I began to view clients as dysfunctional units that needed to be adjusted so that they would function 'properly.' When I talked to experienced practitioners about my feelings, they privately counseled me to focus on what my gut told me to do rather than focusing on regimented techniques given to me by outside authorities.

Most clinicians yearn to be a catalyst for healing for their clients. Many also express frustration with their work due to the rigid limitations in how they believe they are supposed to conduct their therapy sessions. There appears to be a contrast between how therapists want to experience a session and how a session is actually conducted. It is a shame that many graduate training programs do not instill the freedom for their students to pursue innovative and imaginative ways of working. If the truth be told, most graduate supervisors would probably react in horror if they saw their students perform therapy in the manner in which such visionaries as Virginia Satir, Albert Ellis, Carl Whitaker, or Milton Erickson approached their cases.

I can remember attending a workshop conducted by my friend, Dr. Scott Miller, at the 'Evolution of Psychotherapy' conference. In front of thousands of seasoned psychotherapists from around the world, Scott, who is a respected researcher in the area of psychotherapeutic outcome factors, discussed the positive possibilities that the field of psychotherapy could harness by being more open to the traditional and indigenous belief systems of its clients. He advocated working within the belief system of individual clients and becoming comfortable using their ideas about healing combined with one's training to create beneficial outcomes. His information was very well received by the audience.

After his talk, I waited to speak to Scott, who was surrounded by people eagerly sharing with him their use of arcane applications in the privacy of their therapy work. Several spoke in hushed tones as they detailed to Scott how they sometimes used tarot cards or other esoteric aides to help their clients. One woman, with tears in her eyes, told Scott how glad she was that someone as respected as he is in the field gave a voice to therapists who don't want to be limited to the standard methods of interacting with clients. Several others echoed her comment. They were eager to find ways to become, not just a therapist, but a 'healer.'

There have been many researchers who have observed the similarities between traditional healers and psychotherapists. Parallels between the work of healers and therapists have been studied and appear to include similar necessary ingredients for change to occur. These parallels include: the personal qualities of the healer/therapist; the importance of the atmosphere in which the interaction takes place; a shared worldview between client and healer/therapist; and a confiding relationship between client and healer/therapist. There must also be the offering of new information about the client's problem along with alternative approaches in dealing with the problem (Adler & Mukherji, 1995; Cheetham & Griffiths, 1992; Frank & Frank, 1993; Moodley, Sutherland, & Oulanova, 2008; Torrey, 1986).

Healers generally have been viewed as those who treat 'the patient's subjective experience of illness instead of a disease as recognized by biomedicine' (Castillo, 2001, p. 84). These individuals help relieve emotional distress by supplying their clients with a sense of order and understanding about their illness. As a result, clients gain a feeling of control over their illness and have a sense of purpose and meaning that aids in reducing symptoms (Castillo, 2001). Healers create a shift in their clients' self-perception from one of illness and limitation to one of health and possibility. As Hinton and Kirmayer (2017) state:

> healing in the broad sense entails the sense of transformation to a new state and that, in the healing context, whatever promotes change to a new way of being-in-the-world can also function as a flexibility promoter insofar as it increases the ability to shift modes—as well as the awareness of and tendency to make use of this capacity.
>
> *(p. 5)*

I truly believe that most people who become therapists do so because they feel a calling to be healers. They feel a kindred connection with those shamans and wisdom keepers of the past who helped those in need of emotional healing. These healers feel drawn to create transformative experiences, which they believe will help their clients change their lives for the better. They feel a part of the psychotherapy tradition, while only 100 years old, that is profound and offers much to those who suffer. It is similar to that of the physician-healer, whose role is 'to establish connexional relationships with his or her patients and guide them in a reworking of their life narratives to create meaning in and transcend their suffering' (Egnew, 2005, p. 259).

Unfortunately, modern psychotherapy, with the best of its intentions, has failed to be seen by the general public as a transformative healing tradition. In spite of hundreds of thousands of peer-reviewed empirical studies conducted over the past 50 years showing its effectiveness, many people who would benefit from psychotherapy still do not seek it out. It also appears that fewer people are consulting therapists over the last decade. Miller and Hubble (2017) state:

> Epidemiological studies consistently show, for example, most people who could benefit from seeing a therapist don't go to one. And nowadays, fewer people are turning to psychotherapy: 33 percent fewer than did 20 years ago, with most never returning after the first appointment. Not surprisingly, research gathered by the American Psychological Association documents that practitioner incomes have been in marked decline over the same period.
>
> (p. 30)

What is worse is that research shows that many people who enter therapy drop out before any therapy goals have been met. There are a number of reasons for client drop: (1) a lack of experience on the part of therapists; (2) a lack of emotional support; (3) a lack of a therapeutic alliance; and (4) a lack of pre-therapy preparation (Ross & Werbert, 2013). I also believe that another reason for lack of client success is that psychotherapy has ceased to be a 'magical' experience.

Were we to observe the amazing therapists who inspired us as they worked with clients, we would marvel at their skill and creativity. They would appear magical to us and we would hope to obtain that same magic by duplicating their methods. We would then try to learn everything we could about their theories and techniques and attempt to apply those ideas in the same skillful way. There is nothing wrong with this approach in the early stages of our learning to become psychotherapists. The problem is when we mistakenly believe that it is the technique or the theory employed by those masters of psychotherapy that creates the magic in a session.

In the modern era of psychotherapy, there has been an increased focus on technical interventions. This focus often overshadows the importance of the human connection and may even undervalue the need for its presence. Often, therapists identify themselves more with their particular type of therapeutic intervention rather than their role as a facilitator of healing. The recent emphasis on therapies that are deemed 'evidence-based' illustrate the priority that the psychotherapy field has placed on the use of specific technical applications for specific psychological disorders. This rigid emphasis may cause well-intentioned practitioners to overlook the importance of a holistic approach when working with clients. When so much attention is given to specific techniques, it is easy to forget that the crucial aspects to successful outcomes in therapy are connection, caring, and compassion.

THE PSYCHOTHERAPY MARKETPLACE

Lately, there has been an increasing trend in the psychotherapy field in which the marketplace of ideas has become more and more crowded. Every day a new theory, therapy style, or technique is marketed as the latest and the greatest breakthrough. Therapists flock to training programs for these 'new' inventions. This has created thriving businesses for the developers of these programs as the costs of multi-level training programs continue to rise. The good news is that the more these new offerings are marketed, the more new ideas can be heard and explored. The bad news is that the marketing of these programs creates the perception that by learning just the 'right' theory, therapy, or technique, therapists can increase successful outcomes. Some psychotherapy marketers have gone so far as to declare that what they offer is the cure for nearly all emotional problems for which people seek therapy.

A theory is a generalized explanation and a body of knowledge about how a particular subject operates. These generalized explanations are then used to predict and assume outcomes for specific actions. If the theory stands, the results can be consistently replicated by researchers under similar conditions. In the field of psychotherapy, research often seems to promote one different theory of therapy over another. Theory proponents claim that their theory is the most effective and they often have substantial research as evidence of its effectiveness. The rigor shown by these researchers can be impressive and their work has created shifts in, not only the content of educational training, but also funding for public mental health programs.

A good grounding in theory is imperative. However, theories can become cumbersome and limiting if we believe all individuals will automatically fit into our theory. Our clients do not know that they are supposed to respond a certain way at a certain time due to a certain intervention. When the client does not fit the theory of the therapist, the client is then often labeled 'resistant.' When clients are seen as resistant due to their inability to conform to the will of therapists, therapists may become frustrated and angry. They may feel ineffective or burned out due to strict adherence to a theory.

One therapist confided to me that the only real reason he began using his chosen theory of therapy was that it was 'evidence-based.' He had not tried any other form of therapeutic interventions because he believed there was not as much research to back up other theories. He said close to 70 percent of his clients got better using his approach. My question to him was, 'What about the other 30 percent who don't change?' He politely changed the subject at that point.

The great scientist Karl Popper believed that theories by nature are abstract and can only be tested in reference to their implications. Popper asserted that a theory is irreducibly conjectural and brought about by our imagination to solve problems that have come about in a distinct cultural and historical context. He asserted that the truth of any theory cannot be verified by scientific testing. It can only be falsified.

The brilliant family therapist Carl Whitaker once stated that he had a theory that theories are destructive to clinicians. Whitaker argued that too much reliance on a theory can cause a loss of objectivity for each unique person and situation. He believed this could result in a loss of compassion and care for the client. He argued that clinicians should consider giving up strict adherence to theory and become alive as a real person in their sessions. As he eloquently put it, 'Part of the problem is the theoretical delusion that science is curative; that enough knowledge, enough information, the right kind of facts will bring about the resolution of life's doubts, the resolution of all distress' (Neill & Kniskern, 1982, p. 321). This sentiment is echoed by Chenail, Keeney, and Keeney (2015) who state, 'No given theory or technique can be expected to solve the problems of each individual client and his or her own unique experiences.'

It may be difficult to abandon the hope that there is surely one theory or one technique that will help us become superb therapists and help us achieve extraordinarily successful outcomes. Yet, it is important for us to remember that, in spite of the best marketing efforts, research still shows that no one specific therapy application is superior to any other when measuring outcomes. In fact, the most recent research on successful outcomes involves not techniques or theories but shows that success rests on the client's perceptions of the overall progress of treatment and, more importantly still, the key determinant for success still comes down to the client-therapist relationship.

Research has found that when different psychotherapy approaches were compared, there were minimal effect size differences. In spite of how radically different the variety of theories are and how their interventions are in contrast with each other, it was found that all basically had the same effect size. This has become known as the 'dodo bird' effect, named after a character in Lewis Carroll's 'Alice in Wonderland,' who, after a race states, 'Everybody has won and all must have prizes.' These results have caused a shift for many practitioners toward finding the factors involved in creating therapeutic change that are similar in all of the various psychotherapies. These factors, known as 'common factors,' are not connected to one specific model of therapy, but they emphasize the commonality of all the major theories (Duncan, Miller, Wampold, & Hubble, 2010; Greenberg, 2016; Laska, Gunman, & Wampold, 2014; Wampold, 2015).

Evidence was also found that in many cases, nonprofessional therapists often performed as well as experienced clinicians, which casts a shadow of doubt on the effectiveness of specific techniques. In a landmark study by Strupp and Hadley (1979), the efficacy of professional therapists was compared with college professors in working with college students who were suffering from anxiety and depression. The study found that there were no significant differences in outcome between the therapists and the college professors. These results were a shock to many who believed that it was assessment, diagnosing, and specific treatments, along with intensive training on the part of the therapist, which led to successful outcomes. It appeared that the idea that there is a specific knowledge base on alleviating emotional suffering, which only those in the psychotherapy profession possess, is false. As previously stated, subsequent research has shown that this assessment of the therapy field is unfortunately accurate.

This is difficult information for many psychotherapists to hear. Despite years of training, education, and experience, it is possible that someone with very little to no experience as a professional therapist could have just as successful outcomes as a trained and experienced therapist. If this is true, how do we move forward in a field which has spent many decades building an image as the guardians of a base of expertise that others do not have?

In 2006, the American Psychology Association Division of Psychotherapy sponsored a task force whose goal was to determine what really and truly works in psychotherapy. This task force commissioned a series of meta-analysis (a research method that combines the results of multiple research studies into one study) on treatment effectiveness. The results showed that above everything else, the key to successful outcomes in psychotherapy was not a specific technique or theory, but success depended on the strength of the therapeutic relationship.

This task force recommended that clinicians become less restrictive in their work and try to adapt therapy methods to the individual client's characteristics. Norcross and Wampold (2011) unequivocally state that, 'Decades of research now scientifically support what psychotherapists have long known: different types of clients require different treatments and relationships' (p. 131). This is completely in line with what Dr. Milton Erickson was advocating in the 1950s when he told his students, 'Every person's map of the world is as unique as their thumbprint.' Erickson believed a therapist should avoid trying to fit clients into a specific concept or theory.

Essentially, research shows us that, when it comes to successful outcomes in psychotherapy, there is no scientific basis for claiming that any one theory or technique has any more efficacy than others. It has also been found that the variables most associated with effectiveness in treatment are the strength of the therapeutic relationship and personal qualities of the therapist. Clients are best served by therapists who focus on engaging their clients, have the ability to attend to clients' emotional states, and who create strong therapeutic alliances (Feinstein, Heiman, & Yager, 2015; Greenberg, 2016).

For many therapy professionals, the finding that there is little to no difference between specific treatments may seem like bad news, particularly to those who base much of their income on providing certification training programs. From my perspective, this is actually good news. If specific theories, therapies, and techniques are not what makes psychotherapy work, then practitioners can become free from any rigid allegiances in the constant changing psychotherapy marketplace.

Therapists can have more freedom in their work once they realize that what is effective in a session has more to do with the relationship between clients and therapists and the individual qualities they each bring to it. We can then begin to move our profession a step closer to emphasizing 'healing.'

With a renewed interest in the therapeutic relationship and in the individual tailoring of treatment (instead of forcing individuals to conform to the needs of the treatment), therapists have permission to honor their own creativity and clinical intuition. They can move away from the strict adherence to standardized treatments, which can cause disruptions in the therapeutic alliance, while moving toward instinctive interventions that celebrate the uniqueness of the individual client. When this happens, our profession can open the gates to innovative and visionary healing that has eluded us in the past. As LeShan (1996) wisely noted,

> We cannot heal a person by applying a general usage procedure or substance. We cannot manipulate someone into healing. There is no metaphor or method that will serve as a universal elixir for healing. We cannot heal the patient by doing something to him or her ... But we can provide an environment, a specifically designed climate in which this particular patient can flourish. In this environment we, and our relationship with the patient, are a major impact.

(p. 19)

When we are free of restrictive ways of interacting with clients, we can reconnect with the spirit of ingenuity that originally developed the art of psychotherapy. With a proficiency in our therapeutic skills combined with a desire to honor and cultivate the therapeutic relationship, we embody the mind of a scientist and the heart of a healer. We can move our sessions toward adventures in uncharted territory. Opening the doorway to the magical can be frightening if we cling to single-minded and pre-determined perceptions of how therapy should operate. However; it is also inspiring, liberating, and exhilarating as our creative energy expands.

A magical session is one in which both clients and therapists experience a transformational shift. It is a felt sense that happens in the moment and it is difficult to describe. The effects can include a change in how one's body feels as it may suddenly become pleasantly active or relaxed. There may be the energetic sensations of curiosity and playfulness. There may be a powerful change in one's view of situations which previously caused suffering and profound new insights that resonates to the inner core of one's being. The magic might not happen in every session, but it will happen more frequently if preparations are made for such an event to occur. These are the experiences that we wish for, and when they happen, it reinforces our decision to become therapists. We feel more connected to a healing tradition that is alive and inspired.

In the following chapters, there are ideas that I have found to be very useful in generating a magical session. These ideas are not fixed methods to be employed in a methodical manner. These ideas are simply different ways to look at the psychotherapy process which encourages creativity, openness, and healing. Use them and see where they take you as you create your own theory and technique. Become your authority on the best way to do your way of therapy in the moment. Magic abounds for those who seek it.

CHAPTER 2

THE MAGIC OF THE UNKNOWN

Humans have an innate fascination and fear of the unknown. We are drawn to the mysterious, yet we also move away from it because of its hidden nature. Mystery is not for those who want predictability in their lives, for mystery calls us to become accessible to what is not known. However, it is through the unknown that we capture new ideas and from those ideas we grow in new ways. The mysterious inner world of our clients provides us with unique opportunities to explore the unfamiliar, for a magical session is strongly rooted in mystery. In a magical atmosphere, new ideas and actions appear precisely at the right moment, but we may have little clue from where they came. To invite magic into a session, we must welcome the unexpected, for it is from this mysterious space that our best interventions can arise.

Therapists must create this unique space where mystery may appear. This idea of elusive mystery may clash with the notion that the primary focus of therapy is the eradication of pathology. I have found that if the process of therapy is restricted to a focus on pathology, the mystery of the client often disappears. If there is any restriction on allowing the mysterious, we will limit ourselves in what can be useful for clients' healing. When therapy is approached alternatively as an exploration into the mysterious, it is easier for therapists to develop an empathic and collaborative engagement. In this realm, change does not spring from scripted applications, for the heart of the engagement rests on creating relationships that produce more awareness in all involved parties. The magical atmosphere is filled with possibilities and curiosity.

Mystery creates a sense of awe and awe can be a wonderful experience, but it can also be frightening if we are unwilling to welcome it. We never know when the sense of awe will strike us, but we do know that it cannot be forced to appear on command. To celebrate the mysterious allows us to acknowledge that there is something beyond our technical mastery that can help our clients to transcend their problems. If we accept that we may never know what we don't know, we can let go of the relentless pursuit of trying to understand everything. We can help our clients to move from the perspective that life is a problem to be solved, but rather life is an experience by which we may be awed.

Often, therapists purposely avoid delving into mystery in their sessions and make the session as structured as possible to prevent the unexpected from taking place. Treatments follow stringent protocols to protect against spontaneity and the uncharted territory of their clients' inner world. The belief is that therapy must proceed as a strict, calculated endeavor in which no surprises can emerge. This attitude limits the possibility that a magical session may appear. Too much control in the session eliminates any hope of new discoveries, as Johanson and Kurtz (1991) state, 'Mystery is the source of understanding. By definition, we cannot learn from what we already know. That is why so much of psychotherapy is boring. It deals in the stories, justifications, rationalizations, ideas, and theories that we already know' (p. 4).

When we allow the unfamiliar to enter our sessions, we see each client as a unique individual whose inner mystery must be honored, and not limited by the application of template interventions. We also understand that the interventions which were successful with a previous client may not be helpful with our new client and we are compelled to face the uncertainty of the present moment. We can delve eagerly into this new mystery and apply this new knowledge which is more suitable for the present client. Each client becomes an opportunity for the therapist to discover new ways to manifest connection and creativity.

Behind our everyday conscious awareness lies a hidden world which we have difficulty accessing. This mysterious place holds long forgotten memories and emotions which direct our lives to its greatest triumphs and its most painful failures. As therapists, we may find ourselves preoccupied with clients' exterior worlds. We may spend all our time examining our clients' conscious awareness and structure our interventions based on only what we initially perceive based on this conscious information. This way of working can be effective, yet it also can be limiting. If we forget or ignore the hidden world of our clients, then we may make the mistake of labeling certain behaviors which arise from their hidden world as 'resistant' or 'unmotivated.' It might be best to move away from viewing the therapist role of being in control of the session, and instead become a creative agent who allows clients to spend some time drifting into those hidden worlds.

When I was a new therapist, I would often become uncomfortable when my clients drifted from the topic of their problem. I would wonder if perhaps they might be trying to avoid dealing with their issue and might attempting to distract me. I wondered if their reluctance to stay on task was a way for them to not take responsibility for their part in the problem. My mind had been clouded by too much focus on defense mechanisms or obtaining therapeutic goals. At times, it might be best for our clients to drift. The act of drifting often opens up new avenues for therapy to explore, which staying strictly focused on clients' problems might not allow. Magic does not appear in situations where it is expected. Spontaneity is what makes magic come alive. Staying in the same place in a therapy session does not allow any magic to show up. If anything, it can feel confining and authoritarian to clients.

Jillian was a client I was once worked with who taught me the benefit of allowing a session to drift into the realm of mystery. She came to see me for her depression, which she told me had been coming and going for most of her life. After a couple of sessions in which we had altered some of the behavioral patterns she had engaged in, she began to feel her depression encroach upon her. She was a good client who seemed invested in our work. One day I noticed that Jillian kept veering off topic much more frequently than she usually did. I had been having to redirect her back to the topic of examining her thought patterns for any potential limitations to her progress.

Toward the end of the session, Jillian began getting quiet and would gaze out the window for a few moments before continuing our dialogue. At that point, I wondered if she was getting bored of our work or if she was tired. Instead, I felt my intuition tell me to just stay quiet and not redirect her back to our discussion. We sat quietly for a minute or two until Jillian suddenly realized that I had stopped talking to her. She looked at me sheepishly and apologized. I told her that she needn't apologize. I then asked her what she had been experiencing.

Jillian then told me that for some reason she had been thinking about her mother knitting. Jillian's mother had passed away two years earlier. Jillian explained that her mother would sit in the quiet hours of the early evening in her living room and knit. She remembered being a child and laying on the couch silently watching her mother knit. She told me for some reason it brought her comfort to sit in the quiet with her mother. Jillian then glanced off again as she appeared to relive her memory.

My intuition told me to stay silent as Jillian drifted off course. After a minute she looked back up at me and told me that she had never realized when she was a child that her mother may have been depressed as well. She began recalling times in her early childhood when she remembered her mother staying in bed many times and how she sometimes would avoid interacting with other people. Jillian also remembered how her mother had sent her to stay with her grandmother a lot, which at the time was a fun experience for Jillian, but now in her adult years, she saw as a way for her mother to shield Jillian from her mother's depression. Jillian related that as she became a young adult she saw less and less episodes of her mother's depression, but she had wondered if she had still suffered from it in her later years. Tears came to Jillian's eyes as she wondered aloud how her mother had the strength to do the things required of her, be a competent mother, and also deal with the dark world of depression.

After she sat quietly for a few minutes, Jillian suddenly then asked me if I thought she should consider trying to learn to knit. I told her that I could think of no reason why should not do so. Jillian then told me that she wondered that maybe she needed to have more calming soothing activities to help her relax and focus her attention more easily. I again told her that I could so no reason why not. She began to show me a small smile as she told me that after she left her session she was going to check into learning to knit. At that moment our time together had ended and she left with a more positive appearance than she arrived.

When I saw Jillian at our next session two weeks later, she informed me that she had found a 'knitting group.' This group consisted of close to ten women who would get together once a week, drink tea, and teach each other how to knit. The interactions with the group had been good for Jillian who had fun interacting with her fellow group members who were from a variety of ages and backgrounds. She laughed as she said that sometimes the group felt more like a fun sorority than a place for knitting instruction. Jillian had even found she had bonded with an older woman in the group who reminded her a little of her mother. Jillian also stated that she had begun knitting at home in the evening and found that she had started enjoying her evening more as she was focusing on something other than just her depression. Over the next month, Jillian found that she eagerly looked forward to her weekly knitting class, had developed a couple of new friendships, and was experiencing the symptoms of depression less. In time, she found that she needed to come to therapy less often due to her developing new ways of dealing with her negative emotional states.

Jillian's new hobby did more for effectively dealing with her depression than all the interventions which I had attempted to implement. By allowing Jillian to drift without controlling her to a preset agenda, she came to a place where she could find answers for herself. If I had continued to redirect her away from exploring the mystery of her own experiences, then it is doubtful that she would have made such an important and effective shift in her life. My desire to keep her on the path that I had set for her clearly stood in the way for her finding her own way to create positive social interactions and new methods to mindfully sit with her emotions.

In order to grant an available space for the mystery of our client, we must let go of our initial judgment about the world and how one is supposed to react in the world. Our clients' worldview should also be respected and explored before we begin working toward adjusting beliefs that we consider 'irrational' or 'cognitive distortions.' A rush to create a correction in our clients can stifle any possible understanding on our part of how their choices are logical and sensible to them. My greatest therapeutic mistakes usually have been when I believed that I knew better than my clients and then pushed them to acquiesce to my point of view. My desire to be 'right' clouded my perception of what was best for my client. When we quickly act as the 'owner' of objective reality, we often shut down any exploration of clients' interior worlds. The work of Chilean biologist Humberto Maturana casts a shadow of doubt on whether we can ever really know objective reality.

Maturana has done extensive research on the perception of animals, including primates. He found that what an animal visually perceives outside itself has been altered by the retina in a way that is specific to the organization of that animal's nervous system. From this evidence,

Maturana concluded that the animal's perception is not an independent environment being documented by the animal's brain, but instead is mainly determined by the structure of the animal's nervous system, which then determines its reality. Thus, the animals' behavior is entirely determined by the animal's inner world. Maturana believes that the animal's behavior is not fixed, and it can be altered by interactions and experiences. Maturana's work suggests that it is impossible to obtain objective knowledge. All we can really know is a function of the interaction between the outside world and our inner structure, therefore, the interaction between the outside world and our inner world structure creates our reality (Maturana, 1988).

By applying this conclusion to psychotherapy, we can understand that all clients have their own reality in which exists the issue which brought them to therapy. If we try to badger our clients into giving up their reality, then we create resistant clients who fight change. On the other hand, if we understand that clients' perceptions are not distortions of an objective reality, then we can enter their world and find what other mysteries are there to be discovered. To do this, we must let go our belief that what we know is always true. We must be able to let go of the idea that we alone have the correct information which will fix the client. Resistant clients are often created by rigid, dogmatic therapists who lack creativity and who lack the desire to enter the mysterious inner world of the client. As Marks-Tarlow (2014b) asserted, 'To be effective as a psychotherapist means, in part, to honor the mystery of irreducible uniqueness. Although psychotherapists can, in theory, overlook radical uniqueness, they cannot overlook it in practice' (p. 392).

THE MYSTERY OF CLIENT SELF-HEALING

It may be uncomfortable to acknowledge, but it is not the therapist that creates change in clients. Clients are the ones who solve their own problems and find their own resources to effect change in their lives. Therapists are not the sole impetus for change. They simply provide the support so that clients' growth can begin. Therapists may be a catalyst for change to occur, but we should never delude ourselves that it is anyone other than the client who produces the change. We may create the conditions for change to occur, but we can never be solely responsible. This adds yet another dimension of mystery to our work.

Without the efforts of our clients, we, as therapists, can accomplish very little. While some therapists may boast of how they cleverly forced a client to change, in reality, if the client chose not to follow the directives of the therapist, no change would have occurred. The hidden, internal processes of our clients are far too mysterious for us to believe that our ideas and our techniques alone are responsible for clients' transformations. This assumption is silly at best and narcissistic at worst. As McNeilly (2014) states, 'a therapist claiming to change a client is arrogant and even absurd, and that the best that can be attempted is to drift with the client in such a way that in the drifting some internal perturbations can occur with the client that can then sometimes lead to change' (p. 49).

Bohart and Tallman (1999) developed the hypothesis that the therapeutic process only truly works because of the client. To support their assertion, they empirically evaluated the dominant model in psychotherapy, known as the 'medical model.' In this model of psychotherapy, client issues are viewed as comparable with that of medical problems, with the therapist in the role of the medical doctor. Working with client issues from this model first involves a diagnosis. After the diagnosis comes a specific treatment for the specific diagnosis. In the medical model, it is the technique that is of the utmost importance, and any interaction between therapist and client is secondary at best.

As previously discussed, research showed that there are no differences between the variety of techniques or theories, as all appeared to work. The most important ingredients of successful outcomes appeared to be therapist and relationship variables. This has led some to view clients as 'self-healers,' who actively utilized what transpired in a therapy session to create change in their lives. As Bohart and Tallman (2010) state, 'Clients are not submissive recipients of an intervention. They actively operate on therapists' inputs, transforming bits and pieces of the process into information and experiences which, in turn, are used to make change occur' (p. 95).

The interaction between therapist and client creates a shift in the levels of emotional arousal, which could lead to clients accessing their inner resources for healing. Any regimented medical model applied to therapy completely overlooks the mystery our clients bring with them to therapy. Clients make therapy effective as they use what has been offered in the interaction with the therapist in a generative manner to heal.

Clients seek therapy when they believe that they have lost access to their ability to heal themselves. As Bohart and Tallman (1999) state, 'Clients come to therapy when constraints involved in the interaction of themselves with their environment block or disrupt naturally occurring problem-solving efforts sufficiently that the individual gets stuck and is unable to progress on his or her own' (p. 15). If every person carries an 'inner healer,' then perhaps our job as therapists is not to solve the clients' problems, but it is to facilitate the activation of clients' own inner healing mechanism? What if our job is really just to direct our clients so that they are not interfering with their own inner healer? What if our interventions are really just to supply the raw materials which activate our clients' self-healing capability? If our clients are able to solve their own problems, often without us, then perhaps we just need to create an interaction for them that helps them return to their own natural ability as problem solvers.

An example of a self-healing client was a woman with whom I worked named Sandy. She came to see me because she had high levels of anxiety which kept her from focusing on what was important to her. At her first session, Sandy said that she was interested in hypnosis to help her relax. She told me that she had had many traumatic things happen in her life, but she did not want to discuss them. Sandy was very adamant that she did not want to talk about what had transpired in her past. She only wanted to determine if hypnosis would help her in being able to relax. I agreed to her terms of no exploration of her past and we began our work together.

I use an indirect style of hypnosis inspired by the work of Milton Erickson. This method of hypnosis does not direct the client to do anything specific, nor does it make the client submit to any command of the hypnotist. It gives clients options of what they may do if they choose to do so. The importance of this method is that it always gives clients the choice to go into a trance or not. Clients feel more in control and free to respond however they are in the moment. The hypnotherapist is a guide, not a dictator.

I began our session by stating to Sandy that she could relax any way she wanted to do so. I informed her that she was not obligated to relax at all. As our session progressed, she began to relax deeply, and I merely talked to her about how enjoyable relaxation could be. I eventually talked about how people have the ability to move forward in their lives and to leave the pain of the past behind. I commented that each individual is able to make their own choices and to live lives of contentment. I gave no specific commands and did not push Sandy to disclose anything about her past. I made no distinct commentary about her past or what I thought had happened in her past. She had her eyes closed for most of the time and did not say anything nor did she make any unusual gestures. The session lasted for 35 minutes and Sandy appeared to have enjoyed relaxing for that short time.

When I saw Sandy at our next session, she said that she was now feeling calmer throughout her day. She no longer had as many nightmares about her past as she usually experienced. She also told me that she had stopped intensely scratching herself, which she had been doing as a soothing mechanism when her anxiety got to be too much for her. I had no idea that she had been scratching herself nor having intense nightmares. As she thanked me for my help, I could not help but realize how little I had actually done. It was Sandy who found the inner resources to calm her anxiety and to end her scratching. She had self-healed. I was merely a catalyst and witness to that process. To this day, the details of Sandy's past trauma are still a mystery to me, and I honor that mystery.

The greatest mystery we find in our field is the interior world of our clients. This mysterious world is where healing begins. It is not created in our textbooks, in our continuing education training, or in our fancy titles or degrees. This hidden realm holds incredible resources which can heal in ways we could never have imagined. We unleash a magical session when we move past the illogically perceived safety of our treatment plans and instead dive into the dark depths of the unknown.

CHAPTER 3

THE MAGIC OF ALLIANCE

In the majority of studies of psychotherapy outcomes, the role that the therapist plays in the change process is seldom explored. In spite of the therapist being the vehicle from which specific interventions come from, little attention is paid to the importance of therapists' personalities, beliefs, and expectations in the process of psychotherapy. Some researchers have suggested that individual differences between therapists are a fundamental reason that the success rate between therapists varies widely (Blow, Sprenkle, & Davis, 2007; Miller, Hubble, & Duncan, 2008; Wampold, 2006). These variations in success have been reported in field studies with an extensive number of therapists hailing from many different theoretical orientations (Okiishi, Lambert, Eggett, Nielsen, Dayton, & Vermeersch, 2006). Even factors which have traditionally been associated with impacting the quality of the therapeutic engagement, such as training, gender, age, and therapist experience, appear to have little impact on outcomes (Okiishi, Lambert, Nielsen, & Ogles, 2003; Wampold & Brown, 2005). It appears that therapeutic success may have more to do with therapists' individual ability to connect with their clients than any other variables including technique or theoretical orientation.

Anyone who has been a psychotherapist for any length of time intuitively knows that the bond between the client and the therapist is an important aspect for healing. Countless studies have repeatedly shown that a strong connection and collaboration between clients and therapists correlate with more successful therapeutic outcomes.

Norcross (2010) found that over 1000 studies confirmed the relationship between clients and therapists has more impact on outcomes than any specific technique or theory. Magical sessions also do not occur without this connection and collaboration. The warmth and empathy of the therapist, along with a solid feeling of trust on the part of the client, sets the stage for magic to appear in the session. Therapists who are often too quick to attempt to 'fix' their client can appear as if they are not listening to the client, are overly critical or judgmental, or lacking in understanding.

The therapeutic alliance can also be hampered by excessively structured sessions, as well as the therapist's inflexible responses to client input. Also, when the therapist pushes clients into treatment plans which do not fit them, this situation can quickly erode any hope of a magic session. The therapist's ability to intuitively know what technical applications to apply in a session is greatly aided by the therapist's ability to see each client as unique. The honoring of the uniqueness of each client by the therapist strengthens the emotional connections between both parties.

A strong therapeutic alliance helps clients feel they are being understood and cared for, and they will be more willing to complete therapeutic directives. To have an alliance with their clients, therapists need to listen in a way that is nonjudgmental and accepting without being patronizing or inauthentic. There must be a sensitivity to clients' emotional states, as well as supportive attention when clients describe their experiences and worldviews. There is much evidence that the therapeutic alliance may be a substantial aspect of the therapeutic change process. It has been found that the stronger the client – therapist alliance, the greater the improvement in client symptoms at the end of treatment (Horvath & Bedi, 2002; Johansen, Iversen, Melle, & Hestad, 2013; Joyce, Piper, & Ogrodniczuk, 2007; Orlinsky, Rønnestad, & Willutzki, 2004; Priebe, Richardson, Cooney, Adedeji, & McCabe, 2011).

The therapeutic alliance can also provide clients with a platform where they can accept emotional related information about themselves and topics which may be uncomfortable to discuss. Some researchers have even related the creation of a strong therapeutic alliance to the process of constructing secure attachments between children and adults (Schore, 2012; Siegel, 2010; Johnson, 2002). The more clients can trust in the environment, the more they are willing to be open to new information and actions to be taken on their part. As Goldfield (2012) reminds us, 'The therapeutic alliance is not only the glue that keeps clients in treatment, but also a factor that can motivate them to engage in the change process' (p. 20).

In our therapy sessions, we want to have the experience of being committed to our clients while affirming a high degree of empathy. In our communication, we need to be aware of the changes of emotion in our exchanges with clients. We also want to have flexibility and creativity in dealing with any challenges in the session and maintain a sense of competency and effectiveness. Orlinsky and Rønnestad (2005) refer to this way of participating in therapy as 'healing involvement.' The capacity to harness healing involvement requires a sense of advancing in one's skill, but also a willingness to commit to constant improvement. Therapists who are actively engaged in learning more about their own field through professional development and are devoted to moving beyond their present limitations gain more confidence in how they work.

Mental health professionals who have the ability to understand their clients from a multitude of contexts generally have more flexibility in how they respond to those clients. Having a wider consideration for a variety of conceptual contexts enhances the therapists' responsiveness and allows them to more frequently experience healing involvement. Consistently seeking feedback from clients allows therapists to track responsiveness and to make treatment more specific to the individual, which reduces the risk of ineffective outcomes, premature termination, or client drop-outs (Duncan, 2010).

The therapeutic alliance is made stronger when therapists ask for feedback from their clients about what transpired during the therapy session. This one action has shown more effective results in creating more positive therapeutic outcomes (Amble, Gude, Ulvenes, Stubdal, & Wampold, 2016; Lutz, De Jong, & Rubel, 2015). By seeking honest feedback from clients, we demonstrate that we are actively engaged in the therapy, that we value their input in the process, and that we are open to improving the sessions. Feedback also helps us to refine our own focus by giving us a gauge to determine whether treatment goals are being met. Research has shown that therapists who focus on obtaining and utilizing feedback often increase overall effectiveness in their work (Hansen, Howe, Sutton, & Ronan, 2015; Lambert, & Shimokawa, 2011; Miller, Hubble, Chow, & Seidel, 2015; Slone, Reese, Mathews-Duvall, & Kodet, 2015).

Asking for and receiving feedback from clients reinforces the understanding that clients and their therapists are both engaged in a joint effort to resolve clients' issues. This collaborative endeavor requires that both parties agree on the goals for therapy and trust each other in the process. Engaging clients by seeking feedback lays the groundwork that will maintain a reciprocal, interactive relationship as therapy progresses. With this relationship in place, it is much easier to enlist clients in the deliberate work of therapy.

I learned first-hand the importance of seeking feedback when I was a fairly new therapist. I was working with a woman named Cindy, who had come to therapy to help her deal with her grief due to the death of her husband a year earlier. Cindy was a joy to work with since she had a good attitude toward the therapy process and she was willing to openly talk about her grief. We had undergone three sessions together and I believed that we were making progress in our work. Cindy dutifully followed all therapy directives and the homework she was given. I erroneously believed she was really benefitting from my clinical skills. I was wrong.

At the end of our fourth session, I gave Cindy another homework exercise to do, and she appeared to be receptive to what I asked her to do. However, something was gnawing at me concerning how she was really feeling. I wondered if I was just imagining things, but my intuition kept telling me that, in spite of how good everything looked on the outside, Cindy was not doing as well as I thought she was on the inside. I asked how she was feeling and she responded in a positive manner. She said that she always felt better after talking to someone about her grief. It was a nice answer, but I was just not convinced.

I was just about to end our time together, but at the very last moment I realized that I could not just let her leave. I needed to alleviate my own discomfort that something was not quite right. 'Cindy, how do you feel about our session today?' I asked. She smiled and said it was helpful, but she looked down and shuffled her feet a little as she responded. I still believed something was not quite right, so I gently pressed her. 'No, Cindy, really. How was our session today? Did it really give you what you needed? Do you feel it moved you any closer to our goals?' Cindy continued to look down at the floor and stayed silent for a while. Then she said, 'I didn't want to say anything because you seem like a nice man, but even though I feel better talking to you, I think you aren't really hearing me.' I was shocked. I thought I had been listening to her throughout the session and had reflected her statements with empathic understanding.

She continued, 'When we started the session I told you that I felt a little anxious about not going to visit my husband's grave so much. I know you heard what I said, but I just don't think you really got it.' Cindy looked up from the floor and at me. She had been wrestling with how often and how long she stayed at her husband's graveside. She had told me that she was unsure if she was going too often or not going enough. This concern was one of the first things she had said to me in our session and now she felt that I had not adequately dealt with her concern.

Unfortunately, Cindy was right. I had heard her statement about her anxiety over decreasing the time at the cemetery, but I had glossed over it. I had been more interested in discussing her thought patterns about the grave site visits rather than how she was feeling about those visits. I had missed a crucial piece of information in my earnest desire to 'fix' Cindy. At that moment she had not needed me to work on anything, rather she needed me to be present and understanding of her concern. I would have had absolutely no clue about her need if I had not simply asked her about her experience of our session. As soon as I heard her comment, I knew that I had to adjust how I worked with her.

I apologized profusely. She smiled and told me it was 'fine.' But, for me, it was far from 'fine.' 'Cindy, will you please promise me something?' I asked. 'If I can.' Cindy politely replied. 'Will you promise me that in the future you will let me know when you feel you haven't been heard? Will you also tell me if you feel our session is not going well? I want to make sure we make progress, and I really need your guidance to ensure that we achieve our therapy goals.' Cindy smiled and replied that she would be more open with me. I also made a pledge to her that I would seek feedback from her more often. I realized that I had been trying to run the session without the client, and this was not fair nor helpful to her.

Over the next two months, Cindy and I met regularly once a week. I made sure that I asked her about our progress at the end of every session. She then began to share more of her own inner thoughts with me and we began to co-create a positive therapeutic outcome. We were building momentum and the energy in the therapy room was much different since we both felt more engaged, energized, and invested in our work together. Merely asking for feedback from Cindy changed the dynamics of the therapy session. She felt a part of the therapy process. Therapy was done with her, not to her. At the end of the two months, Cindy told me that she was in a good place to begin her new life and decided to end her therapy. We had both benefitted from our time together. I learned to overcome my own hesitancy to ask for feedback and possibly hear things I might not like to hear. I also saw the critical value of seeking client feedback. I now see feedback as a very necessary aspect of transformative psychotherapy.

Feedback allows clients to become the guides in the therapy process. It allows them to lead their therapists into unexplored territory that is most in need of their therapists' attention. Getting feedback and then acting on it requires that therapists listen even more deeply to their clients' own perceptions and explanations of where they are in their lives. Feedback also helps to create more a personalized approach to how therapists respond to their clients. Seeking client feedback creates a way for clients to feel they are a part of the therapy process. They become more active in determining the resolution to the problems which motivated them to enter therapy.

PRESENCE

One of the most important ways to set the stage for therapeutic magic is for therapists to bring a sense of presence into their sessions. When there is a therapeutic presence, we are completely present, and we also allow a space for our own humanity. Presence may be the most necessary ingredient in creating change in therapy. It is the putting aside of our preconceptions and being open to the experiences of our clients. We must look past our assumptions about people and welcome each client as a unique individual. We need to bring our whole self to the interaction and put away any prepossessed goals for the engagement.

The great existential psychotherapist, James Bugental (1989), believed there were three aspects needed for presence: being open to the client's experiences, allowing for one's own experiences, and responding to the client from our own experience. When we have presence in our work, we give our clients, as well as ourselves, permission for and a safe place to experience all aspects of emotion. The relational interaction creates an environment of connection and affirmation. To embody presence, 'requires that the caregiver have skills of centering, intentionality, intuitive knowing, at-one-ment, imagery, and connection' (McDonough-Means, Kreitzer, & Bell, 2004, p. S–25). Therapeutic presence has also been seen as a 'complex mix of appreciative openness, concerted engagement, support, and expressiveness' (Schneider, 2015, p. 305).

The importance of presence is certainly not a new idea in psychotherapy for luminaries such as Carl Rogers, who was writing about the importance of presence in working with clients as far back as the 1950s. Indeed, it is difficult to fathom how the therapeutic alliance can be effective without the therapists' presence. Unfortunately, it appears that there is less focus on this crucial factor in therapy training and workshops. Most psychotherapy conferences appear to focus on what therapists are 'doing' to a client, rather than how therapists are 'being' with a client. The lust for technique can often overtake even the most seasoned practitioner when the glitter of the latest and greatest new technical application appears. However, those techniques will always work better when therapists have spent an equal amount of time on developing their therapeutic presence. As Schneider (2015) states, 'The cultivation of presence is key to therapeutic healing. We've relied too long on the verbal and procedural aspects of therapy, all the while overlooking the organic hub of formally identified therapeutic factors' (p. 304).

It can be difficult to teach the art of presence to therapists in training. Presence is more than silence and attentiveness for even a highly engaged conversation can have presence. Presence can even be in the middle of a confrontational moment with a client. It is a sense of absorption in what is happening in the moment. It is mindfulness in action, an awareness of sensations and experiences occurring in the present. It is a way of interacting with the spontaneous nature of life.

Unfortunately, too many therapists have come to see mindfulness only as a therapeutic technique for the client. If the therapist's focus is on the implementation of mindfulness as a technical application, then having a mindful presence with clients can often be difficult. Some have even observed that, 'In the evidence-based practice movement, presence is too often viewed as something one performs in order to comply with quantitatively determined protocols' (Schneider, 2015, p. 306). Rather than merely viewing mindfulness as a technique for clients to calm their anxiety or examine their depression, therapists might want to apply this to themselves. Mindfulness does not always mean sitting quietly while one detaches from one's streams of thought. Mindfulness can also be experiencing the essence of the moment shared with one's client. In their rush to be effective and results-oriented, therapists would be wise to remember that research stresses the importance of the relationship between client and therapist in generating positive outcomes (Norcross & Wampold, 2011). Maintaining the connection and the sense of presence with clients is a vital element to ensuring a strong therapeutic relationship.

Throughout the world, in a variety of healing traditions, it is common for people to perceive a special presence exuded from powerful healers. This special presence is 'capable of inducing an experience of recovery, wholeness, peace or well-being in people who suffer' (Jonas & Crawford, 2004, p. 751). This healing presence is noticeable by all who experience it. Many healing traditions have believed that this special quality 'operates outside the bounds of conventional psychosocial dynamics' (Jonas & Crawford, 2004, p. 751). This healing presence is common to both current Western models of healing and to those of indigenous traditions (McCabe, 2008).

When presence is embodied by therapists, they are essentially performing the same practice as those ancient healers and shamans, whose mere presence energized and encouraged changes in their clients. Studies of indigenous healers have also shown the importance of practitioners possessing charisma and a healing presence, which, if not displayed, may diminish their ability to effectively work with their community. Much like the research of therapist qualities on psychotherapy outcomes, it has also been conjectured that it is the personality of these indigenous healers that was the most important aspect of the healing process and not their specific techniques or system of working (Krippner, 2012).

Much like indigenous healers, the healing presence of a mental health practitioner is often characterized by empathy, being focused on and attentive to the client, having compassion for those who are suffering, and a charismatic presence which may be both inspiring and motivating (Frank & Frank, 1993, McDonough-Means, Kreitzer, & Bell, 2004). One must not underestimate the power of charisma on the part of the therapist. I am not referring to charisma in the sense of being manipulative or narcissistic, but rather as a way of being that makes other people feel comfortable and connected. Charisma can be described as one's ability to exhibit warmth toward others while being perceived to be able to exert control of his or her environment (Cabane, 2013).

Frank and Frank (1993) found that a particular striking quality for an effective therapist is the ability to be charismatic. Heide (2013) asserts that charisma can be an important quality that therapists can call upon to be more effective in their work. A therapist's ability to be engaging and expressive can aid in motivating and inspiring clients to move beyond their presently perceived limitations. Da Silva (2008) found that these qualities were positively correlated with higher measures of client satisfaction.

When one thinks of many of the celebrated therapists in the modern history of psychotherapy, most all of them had a charismatic quality to them. When one watches videos of these great therapists working, it is easy to see why their clients felt they were so effective. Seeing masters such as Virginia Satir sculpt her clients while she beams at them, Carl Whitaker as he playfully cajoles parents who are enabling their children, Albert Ellis getting clients to sing silly songs about their fears, and Carl Rogers masterfully supporting clients with his deep compassion, present a connecting thread of charisma and presence between all these masters that impacted the people who worked with them.

I am a firm believer that if there is no healing presence on the part of the therapist, then there will be no magical session. The field's quest for technical proficiency often overlooks the personal qualities that therapists themselves bring to their sessions. The focus on performing technical applications over the presence of the therapist may be one reason why researchers find little evidence that experienced therapists achieve better outcomes than inexperienced therapists (Tracey, Wampold, Lichtenberg, & Goodyear, 2014). When we allow a space for presence, we can fully accept all the experiences which emerge in the interaction. We are open to these experiences and permit them to be what they are without attempting to control them. Our own responses, which develop out of the present moment, allow us to obtain information, intuition, and inspiration from our inner world. We can reach out to our clients when we allow ourselves to be vulnerable and available. Even while we remain grounded, we can still feel a sense of absorption in the mysterious worlds of our clients.

The sense of presence means we are centered and this centered state allows for what is happening now in the immediacy. In the therapy dance with clients, presence is the balance between having too close of an involvement and too much distance. When an inflexible agenda has been established by the therapist, it is much more difficult to experience presence. Presence allows for whatever may happen in the moment and what clients feel is important to emerge. Being receptive to what is alive and spontaneous helps to maintain a sense of presence. Having a sense of curiosity as we listen to the stories of our clients often creates opportunities for therapeutic magic. Being fully focused and emotionally attuned to clients' concerns about their issues and the therapy process can also help in alleviating client resistance toward future interventions. Westra, Constantino, and Aviram (2011) found that simply being more understanding and empathic in the first session toward clients viewed as resistant led to increased outcome expectations in those clients.

Staying present and attending to our own emotional state can decrease distractions and increase the interactive flow in therapy. As Geller and Greenberg (2012) state:

> Preparing for presence involves taking the time to clear one's self of personal issues, self-needs and concerns, judgments, preconceptions, plans, and conceptualizations so that the therapist can create room inside to take in the experience of the client. It involves emptying out from the self-unwanted distractions so that the therapist can enter freely into the session with the client. To enter into the session in this way allows the therapist to discover the unique experience of the client at that particular moment in time.
>
> *(p. 85)*

Presence is not something that can be completely articulated through language. I have found that when there is presence and a connection between people, there are often periods in which no words need be spoken. Although I have a deep love for words (reading and writing are two favorite activities) and having studied the importance of linguistics in psychotherapy, I also realize there are limitations to language in effectively expressing what one feels. A felt sense can be difficult to explain in words. Sometimes, therapists pressure their clients for appropriate labels for what they are feeling. We might do better to just allow them to feel what they may without requiring identification of their experiences. Perhaps there is a belief that the only way to help clients is to have all the pertinent emotional labels. However, pushing clients to move too quickly from unconscious embodiment to conscious descriptions can decrease the magic of the interaction. Pushing for too much narrative too soon can invade and rob clients of the privacy of their own inner worlds.

Often, we cram too much verbalization into an interaction, and this verbal tennis match is really only our attempt to avoid the intimacy of silence and connection. Silence can create a sense of discomfort in us. We fear being open to the other person in that moment. Complete openness to everyone we meet is not desirable, but we could try to deepen our connection to those about whom we care. Today, silence and connection are rare commodities for our attention and emotions are distracted and manipulated by a variety of triggers. It is any wonder that many people attend meditation retreats where vows of silence are taken, forcing them to connect somehow without words? A magical therapist should be warned, however, for sitting in silence and connection creates an environment that invites into the open such 'dangerous' emotions as creativity, inspiration, freedom, and love.

I remember sitting in a therapy session with a client who had been listening as I talked about her situation. We had actually worked together for quite a while and she had made a bit of progress, but she was still trying to find that elusive something which would give her peace in her life. In some ways, she felt defeated by life, but she still held out hope that life could be different and better. As I spoke to her, she stared down at the floor. I gave her my insight into how we were progressing in our therapy work, but at that point, I became aware of a feeling that I might be directing her too much. With this feeling in mind, I told her that I had a great deal of trust in her and how she would approach her problems. I also said that I would be available to assist her. I let her know that I was no longer going to direct her toward what she needed to do because she intuitively knew the best thing for her. I also said that I knew she could and would change when she was ready and that I would support her ideas of what she felt was best. When I finished speaking, silence hung in the air. She appeared frozen and continued her downward gaze. I really did not know what else to say so I just allowed the moment to unfold. Silence reigned in the therapy room.

She eventually looked up directly into my eyes. In the next few moments, without any words being exchanged, we shared the process of her changing at a deeply personal level. Our eyes conveyed all that was needed. What probably only lasted a few minutes seemed like an hour of expansive openness as she and I moved together through the fields of wordless connection. Tears formed in her eyes as she had made the necessary connection at the unconscious level to find freedom from her emotional pain. Without any dialogue exchanged between us, I could sense when she began to mentally move beyond the pain of the past. I sensed that she could now allow herself to enter the present moment of peace and new life. Any request for a description of what she was feeling on my part would have robbed her of that precious moment. My intuition told me that what she needed in that moment, more than anything else, was just my presence. I held a space for her so that she could dive into the depths of herself.

Authenticity

Our clients know very quickly if we are truly authentic. Most clients sense whether they can trust us within the first few minutes of a therapy session. If we are masquerading as someone we are not, it will not take very long for clients to pick up on that discrepancy. If we struggle to give a false impression, then the struggle will easily be seen by others. Our desire to express compassion and caring for our clients cannot be forced or contrived. These expressions have to be authentic.

Authenticity is not the specific conscious actions we take, but rather it comes from the essence of who we are. At its core, authenticity 'is the ability to be touched, surprised, changed – all in the relationship with the other – while keeping touch with one's own inner experience and interpretations and forming a personal point of view' (Schnellbacher & Leijssen, 2009). Therapists who are authentic avoid facades and they are willing to share their own inner experiences at appropriate times. Their interaction with clients does not imitate other therapists and their therapeutic interventions are not based on prearranged patterns of engagement. Authentic therapists generally have a higher awareness of self. They stay grounded in the present moment while still being emotionally involved in their clients' narratives (Yalom, 2002).

Clients will place more value, not on the specific things we say, but how we are as human beings. How we express our character is a crucial part in the creation of a working alliance. The more genuine we are with ourselves, the more we can benefit our clients. Rest assured, however, we can truly be ourselves and still maintain our standing as a professional, for our authenticity is never at the expense of our clients. When we are authentic, we also take responsibility for our thoughts, words, and actions. We are aware of our own internal experiences and are willing to share them with our clients.

When psychotherapists are authentic, they can act with integrity. They will be cognizant of the motivations behind the actions they take in sessions. This authenticity frees them to become more creative and frees them from a fixed mindset that is closed to hunches, feelings, and intuition. Being free means set assumptions and beliefs will give way to a new openness to clients' experiences and new understandings. Authentic therapists become less afraid of spontaneous maneuvers in their work. They recognize the absurdity in life and do their best to embrace the paradoxes of living in such a world. They are honest about their own experiences while exhibiting professional poise in their interactions.

In order to exhibit authenticity, we first need to deal with our fears of not being competent enough, not being in control, and not having approval. We need to be willing to allow all the things we may have worried about to actually show up. We have to let go of our preconceptions of how a session should progress. We have to allow for the unexpected to happen and to even encourage its appearance. The renowned existential philosopher Martin Heidegger believed that having authenticity was all about being open to what life brings, including our own impending deaths.

It takes bravery to be who we really are, particularly when we are working with clients, for it can be anxiety provoking to sit and feel with the often-distressing emotions that can occur in our sessions. However, if we allow ourselves to fully be with those experiences, then we provide an example of how to do so for our clients. We want our clients to feel that they are supported and safe when they are with us. Our quiet acceptance then becomes a model.

Often, we have to take time to really examine ourselves. If there is something that bothers us about a client, it may be that the client represents what we either reject or fear. One of the most important functions of being congruent with the client is establishing trust. When we do not hide our thoughts and feelings, we act a true desire to help our clients. Being aware of our nonverbal behavior, and any potential incongruity with our words, is critical when developing trust with our clients. If we are unaware of how our clients perceive us, we can often derail any assistance we can give them. When we pretend that we don't have an emotion or avoid emotion altogether, this does little to provide an environment of trust in the therapy room. If there is no trust, then there will be no magical session.

I remember one day sitting in the office waiting for a client. I observed one of my colleagues, Jean, walk with her client, an older woman, to the exit to say goodbye. They both said the usual pleasant things and the client left. Jean then came and sat down beside me. She told me that she was stuck with this client. She did not think she could get the client to follow simple directives that could help her. Jean wondered out loud why it was so difficult to work with this woman.

'It's simple,' I said. 'How so?' she asked obviously taken aback by my comment. I replied, 'You don't like her and she knows it.' Jean started to say something and then stopped. She was quiet for a few moments. 'How could you tell?' she asked. I answered, 'I could tell because your body language was incongruent with what you were saying.' 'You didn't act as if you liked her. It was obvious to me and I am pretty sure it is obvious to her as well.' She slowly nodded. 'What don't you like about her?' I asked curiously.

Jean's face became stern as she exclaimed, 'She's a snob! She thinks she's better than everyone else. I hate working with her. I wish I could work with someone who was less haughty.' 'So you wish you could only work with people who are not haughty?' I inquired. Jean reluctantly smiled and nodded. I commented, 'Well, it is kind of haughty for you to exclude people who you think are haughty, isn't it?' Jean stopped smiling as I continued, 'I'm not trying to judge you, but I think there might be something about haughtiness that causes you to react so strongly. I don't care for haughty people either, but it seems to have a grip on you.' We ended our short chat and went on with our day.

Later that day Jean appeared in my office door and said with a smile, 'Mom issues.' 'I hadn't thought about it in a long time, but when I was a teenager, my mother would sometimes put down some of my friends in what I perceived as a haughty manner. I guess something about my client reminded me of my turbulent teenage years.' She told me that, in spite of loving her mother, Jean was often angered and embarrassed by her mother's haughtiness. She had come to realize that it was her mother's own insecurity that caused her to raise a snobbish front when dealing with people. Jean told me that she needed to start working on putting to rest her own feelings about her mother's pretension.

Jean continued to work on her 'mom issues' over the next few weeks, and I noticed a change in the way she greeted and said goodbye to her haughty client. What was even better was that, in time, I also noticed a change in how her client responded to Jean. What had previously been a very formal greeting and farewell, now became a close connection of warm smiles and appreciation. When Jean examined her own feelings, she could be more congruent with her client, this helped the client let down her own facade of haughtiness.

Our clients are often very willing to overlook our fallibility and mistakes if they sense that we are being genuine. Our attempts to motivate clients' full participation in therapy is increased when we present ourselves as we really are. If we are frustrated with clients, sometimes it is important to let them know we are frustrated with them. As long as we share our feelings in a manner that is neither destructive nor demeaning, we can actually grow the therapeutic relationship by articulating frustrations and irritations. We also model to our clients how to effectively share one's personal feelings. Our openness will usually result in more openness from our clients. Our being authentic encourages their authenticity.

EXPECTANCY

Expectancy serves as a way to predict what will happen as a result of our actions, and these predictions often give us a feeling of control over our environment. Much of our daily life is governed by our expectations about what could happen to us. Many of these expectancies have become conditioned beliefs formed by past experiences.

Expectancy is a person's appraisal of the likelihood that a certain outcome will occur. If we expect to have a pleasurable experience, we naturally move toward that outcome. However, on the other hand, we automatically move away from an experience in which we expect to receive pain. Our minds and bodies respond according to the expectancy that we have about potential outcomes. There are cases in which people have manifested pain in a situation where there was no reason, the pain came because they had a very strong expectation of feeling the sensation of pain. Our expectation can become a self-confirming process.

The importance of a person's expectancy has been noted in many research studies. The role of the placebo has shown over and over again that people's expectations can have major effects on both psychological and physical health. Many medications, which had success in clinical trials, were discovered to be no more effective than placebos. When participants in control groups expected to experience a specific medication, and instead received placebos, they often displayed the positive effects (and the side effects) of the medication.

According to the proponents of the expectancy theory of motivation, people will pursue a goal as long as there is an expectation that they can reach the goal. This is true in psychotherapy as well. If someone is grappling with depression and believes that there is little that he or she can do to alleviate his or her suffering, this expectation may prevent him or her from taking any action that could change the depression. There is also the possibility that if the person's expectancy is that the depression cannot be helped, this mindset may very well sabotage any action they do take to change his or her emotional state.

Frank and Frank (1993) assert that for any therapy work to be effective, clients must have an expectation of hope that change can happen. It is the restoration of hope which leads to a desire to change that brings transformational change in therapy. Many researchers believe expectancy is strongly related to positive outcomes in psychotherapy; however, many therapists often undervalue its importance (Constantion, Penek, Bernecker, & Overtree, 2014; Greenberg, Constantino, & Bruce, 2006; Holtforth, Kreiger, Bochsler, & Mauler, 2011; Rutherford, Wagner, & Roose, 2010). Investigation into the healing practices of shamans found that the expectancy of the person receiving the treatment is of the utmost importance. The shamans who have been found to be most effective at their work often utilized the hope and expectations of the people who sought them out to maximize success (Krippner, 2012).

With such an important part of the human experience based on expectancy, we, as therapists, need to focus on giving our clients hope and the positive expectation of change from the first moment we meet them. The primary reason our clients come to us for therapy is that they have lost all hope. They have no expectation that their situation will change. They feel locked in place and unable to move forward in their lives. If they believed that change was going to take place before they came to us, they probably would not seek psychotherapeutic help. Their belief that things will never change has led them to feelings of helplessness, which quickly spirals into hopelessness. They become stuck in a vicious circle of negative events, negative behaviors, and negative actions which reinforce each other.

In order to promote a solid therapeutic alliance in the beginning stages of therapy, therapists might consider the value of exploring the expectations that clients themselves have of the therapy process. This is more than just the establishing of goals, this exploration can give therapists information about how clients perceive therapy will help them, and what are the clients' perceptions of the therapist. Discussing clients' future expectations of outcomes, their beliefs about how therapy will proceed, and their feelings about the therapist can result in a stronger alliance that ultimately results in better outcomes (Patterson, Anderson, & Wei, 2014). As Kirmayer (1999) states, 'To evoke strong positive expectations, the clinician must provide a treatment that fits expectations or otherwise invoke personally and socially powerful forms of authority' (p. 453).

A critical part of any psychotherapy treatment is the incorporation of a process in which clients will notice therapeutic change. Clients need to see that change is happening, even if they do not fully understand why that change is taking place. Noticing change not only gives clients confidence that the treatment is working, but it also bolsters a sense of hope that the future will be better. Since clients often have a sense of hopelessness about their problems, it is imperative that we work toward enhancing their expectations that there is indeed hope. A magical session is one in which the atmosphere of positive expectation fills the air.

Directions to notice change can be specific or nonspecific. Directing a client to watch for some change between sessions, no matter how small, can go a long way toward moving their attention away from hopelessness. Insisting that there will be a change during the therapy process, even though you don't know what it will be, can be uplifting and affirming to clients whose expectations have been less than hopeful. Focusing on a hopeful future can give clients a feeling of optimism that change will come. Optimism goes a long way toward fostering a sense of resiliency and a feeling of some control over one's life.

In order to shift awareness from hopeless scenarios to possibilities of change, we must make sure that we do not become overwhelmed by our clients. It is very easy to become hypnotized and paralyzed by all the baggage that people bring with them to therapy. However, if we are grounded and present during the unpacking of such baggage, our clients know that we are there to help them and to believe that change can take place. This gives an image of competence and the appearance of dependability to our clients, while helping build positive expectancy. If therapists appear less than confident, then their ability to achieve positive outcomes may be in jeopardy. As Ackerman and Hilsenroth (2003) state:

> The ability of a therapist to instill confidence and trust within the therapeutic frame is essential to therapeutic success. Related to the development of these ideals is the therapist's capacity to connect with the patient and convey an adequate level of competence to effectively help patients under distress. Moreover, the therapist's attributes similar to dependability, benevolence, and responsiveness are expected to be related to the development and maintenance of a positive alliance. It is also expected that therapist's confidence in their ability to help his/her patients will be related to a positive alliance.
>
> *(p. 4)*

I had one client who brought with her one of the largest sets of emotional baggage I had ever experienced. Once our session started, she began to tell me about the early trauma she had been through, her multiple abusive relationships, her previous experiences with addiction, and her psychiatric hospitalizations. There were so many tales of emotional ordeals and personal hardships that I could feel myself becoming overwhelmed by all of this intense information. I had to work very hard to keep my poker face intact so she would not notice my discomfort.

When she came to the end of her long tale of misfortune and pain, she intently looked at me. I remember asking, 'Is there anything else?' She said to me that there wasn't any other information. I then replied, 'Oh good, I was hoping this wouldn't be one of those tough cases.' She looked surprised and asked me, 'Do you think you can help me?' I smiled and told her. 'The information you gave me leads me to believe that we can do some really good work together.' She smiled and then sighed. 'I am so glad to hear that. I tried going to two other therapists and they both seemed overly affected by my story. One even told me that she was concerned that she could not adequately help me.'

We began to work together and had some small successes. One day she told me that my comfort with her story, treating it as something that could be helped, gave her a feeling of confidence that she would get better. Her previous interactions with the other therapists had left her feeling as if she were broken. To this day, I still believe that my interventions with her were not what made the difference. The primary catalyst for her change was that, for the first time, she had hope for her future. Once she saw that someone else believed that there could be positive change, she bought into the process.

A magical session needs to begin with the expectation that things can be different. We cannot count on our clients to have this expectation when they begin therapy. We, the therapists, need to set the intention for change. We need to be aware of how easy it is to drift back into impoverished narratives from the past with our clients, instead of striving toward future positive outcomes. By instilling in our clients the belief in the achievability of treatment goals, we set the groundwork for clients to embrace a new expectancy, and this will lead to better outcomes. As discussed earlier, people will only seek to reach a goal that they think they can get.

I love the types of questions that solution-oriented therapies encourage asking clients. These questions automatically direct clients' minds toward the future possibility for change, instead of the present perception of cemented, unchanging problems. The use of such phrases as 'before you begin to change,' 'after you begin to change,' and 'when you begin to change,' direct our clients' minds toward a future of positive outcomes. Therapy needs to have a future orientation more than only a past or present orientation. In the history of psychotherapy, some of the earliest therapies focused only on past focused dialogues. Conversation was solely about clients' histories and they were treated to intense psychological archaeology. Therapists attempted to dig up a root cause for clients' distress. Years later, the 'present focused' therapies were in vogue where only what the client experienced in the present moment was explored. More recently, psychotherapy has been focusing on co-designing positive future outcomes with less emphasis on client deficits and more emphasis on client strengths.

One of my mentors always gave her clients a task in their first session. They wrote a letter to themselves from their future self. She would tell clients to imagine themselves five years in the future and to write a letter about how they have positively changed. She then asked clients to describe in detail how good they would feel in five years knowing that their problems had been solved. She directed them to use vivid imagery to describe the emotions that they would be feeling in five years. Clients would be asked to bring the letter to their next therapy session and read them aloud to her. She found that this one task helped her gain more cooperation and a sense of shared expectancy for a positive outcome. This task also allowed her to determine if clients were clear in their goals.

It is so important to produce an environment of possibilities which can give hope to our clients. If clients do not believe things can change, it can often be a struggle to persuade them that their lives can be different. If all we can do is give them hope, that hope can be enough to create change. As Horowitz (2008) states, 'Hope is nurtured and cultivated, growing out of the transformation of dimly imagined possibilities into realities. It exists not in the abstract but in the relationship that comes to life over the course of therapy. Hope is indissolubly tied to expectation' (p. 238). A magical session is one in which there is a future orientated to the creation of a positive transformation in clients' lives. Sometimes when clients do not have faith, we must have the faith for them.

CHAPTER 4

THE MAGIC OF
AN EXPERIENCE

Being a witness to the transformation of a client in a therapy session is a stirring and uplifting experience for any psychotherapist. This magical moment is a high point of any therapy session. Both therapist and client can literally feel the shift that takes place, but they often find it hard to put words to the experience. However, these experiences reaffirm our original desire to enter the psychotherapy field and we eagerly look forward to the next time a transformation may take place. For many therapists, these experiences are fleeting due to their approach to their therapy sessions. If sessions are scripted 'by the book,' and the same applications are used on every client that they see, then the likelihood of having such moments become more and more unlikely.

Psychotherapy is traditionally conducted through the use of conversation. The conversation between the therapist and client is intended to guide the client toward changing, and since its inception, psychotherapy has been known as the 'talking cure.' This perception of therapy as completely focused on talking often gives the impression that it is *only* the information that the therapist gives to the client that facilitates change on the part of the client. It doesn't take one long in a therapy career to discover that receiving information by itself does not guarantee with any certainty the activation of change in clients. In fact, it is not uncommon to find that clients already possess the very information therapists are prepared to give them. I assert that it is not the information alone which causes magical shifts in clients, but rather it is the 'experience' of being in therapy which brings about change. Either consciously or unconsciously, clients come looking not just for new information, but for an out of the ordinary experience.

Throughout history, people have been intrigued by the power that an experience has to transform lives. In many cases, people have been completely changed due to one intense experience, whether a good one or a bad one. Neuroscience has shown us that our brains can change as a result of challenges in our environment. For many years, it was believed that humans only had a limited number of neurons in the brain. Now, researchers have determined that the creation of new neurons, called 'neurogenesis,' can occur throughout a person's life, and it is through experience that these neurons can form. These new neurons are often associated with memory and plasticity, a process which generates modifications in our neuronal connections. An intense experience strengthens or weakens such connections (Cappas, Andres-Hyman, & Davidson, 2005).

Rossi (2001) believes that, 'The essence of psychotherapy becomes a process of facilitating "creative moments" that are encoded in new proteins and neural networks in the brain' (2001, p. 155). Providing information to clients in itself does little to initiate creative moments. In order to activate any change in our clients' brains, we will need to provide an experience which activates new growth and new connections of neurons. From this perspective, psychotherapy is not simply about giving new information to clients, instead, it is about providing information in an emotionally compelling manner. Essentially, clients will feel their session is magical only if they have had a compelling new experience. These experiences can change clients as they learn alternative ways to feel and think about their problems. Many feel that 'emotional experience is a central object of attention in psychotherapy' (Voutilainen, Peräkylä, & Ruusuvuori, 2010, p. 85).

In order for clients to have a magical experience, it is important to be aware that certain conditions in the session need to be in place. One of the most important is that therapists should have the ability to modulate between higher and lower levels of emotional arousal within the session. In order to begin the process of change, some clients may need to be emotionally activated if they are presently under-aroused, while others, who are over-aroused, may need help in reducing their overactive emotional state (Casper & Berger, 2012). Therapists who are comfortable with varying degrees of emotional exchanges are generally more effective in accessing and utilizing clients' emotions for the benefit of the session.

Originating in the oldest parts of the brain, 'emotion is fundamentally adaptive, making it possible for people to process complex situational information rapidly and automatically in order to produce actions appropriate for meeting important organismic needs (e.g. self-protection, support). Emotion is central to human function, dysfunction and change, and thus an appreciation of the forms, structure, and variety of emotion processes is an essential basis of practice' (Elliot & Greenberg, 2007, p. 243). Clients come to therapy due to emotionally distressing events in their lives, in their past or present. In order to have the most impact in our sessions, 'Therapists must elicit an affectively engaging experience that changes the emotional meaning of an event' (Armstrong, 2015, p. xv).

Most of the patterns we have learned, and unconsciously use, are saved in what LeDoux (1996) refers to as the 'emotional brain,' located in the midbrain between the brain stem and the cortex. This part of the brain learns from intense experiences and repetition. It often overrides the logical and rational part of our brain, the neocortex, with previously learned patterns of responding. These patterns continue operating until we intervene with a new experience that is intense.

The emotional brain is where our emotional memories and habitual behaviors reside. This part of the brain could be thought of as our 'unconscious' due to our lack of awareness of how our unconscious brings about our responses to certain situations and experiences. This part of the brain does not process information in the same way as our neocortex. In fact, the emotional brain 'speaks a very different language from the neocortex, which is more word and logic oriented' (Armstrong, 2015, p. 11).

It is through our neocortex that we process information through analysis, logic, and language, but it is in the emotional brain that we process information through experiential schemes. A scheme is a set of organizing principles manufactured from the clients' past experiences which interact with their current life situations. These are models from which clients construct how they respond to future interactions. Since these schemes are mostly unconscious and nonverbal, it is often very difficult to change these patterns through the use of logic and verbal reasoning only. As much as thought and logic are a part of our lives, the emotional aspect of our experiences is equally prevalent in our choices. It is our emotions that register patterns in our environment and direct our orientation to the world around us (Greenberg & Paivio, 2003).

Our goal for a magical session is to set the stage for an experience that will change unconscious learning associated with an emotional pattern. As Voutilainen et al. (2010) observe, 'the processes through which the therapeutic change takes place might not have so much to do with gaining new insights or rationality but with new experiences of emotional expression and response in the therapeutic relationship – which are then supposed to transform the patient's ways of relating to others and his or her own experience' (p. 86). With this in mind, it is only logical to contend that if these habitual patterns are held in place by emotions, then 'it is only through accessing emotion and emotional meaning that emotional problems can be cured and that purely rational methods, although sometimes useful, too often do not cure distressed emotion. Reason has never succeeded in controlling passion' (Greenberg & Paivio, 2003, p. 4).

Clients can become stuck in and influenced by patterns that have habitually occurred over many years. These patterns are reinforced and maintained by the self-reflexive nature of human awareness (Bateson, 1971; Burns & Engdahl, 1998; Finlay & Gough, 2008, Leary & Tangney, 2003). Any experience of responding to older patterns in a new, emotionally intense way provides evidence to clients that new actions are possible for them and that older patterns can be altered. When we help our clients to have new emotional experiences different from their usual responses, we are providing opportunities for them to know that they are more flexible than they previously thought. The change in their emotions and behaviors signal to them that they are capable of breaking the spell of their habitual patterns of interaction.

Having emotionally engaging interactions that are different from what clients have experienced in their past, opens the door to the possibility of new client responses in the future. It is through this engagement that 'the therapist helps clients understand and transform their emotion schemes through empathic listening, evocative or expressive interventions; therapists also help clients reflect on and reevaluate emotion schemes and expose themselves to more adaptive emotional responses' (Elliot & Greenberg, 2007, p. 243). When habitual patterns are interrupted, it allows creative moments to emerge (Rossi, 2002).

The results of these interactions are sometimes referred to as 'corrective experiences,' in which 'a person comes to understand or experience an event or relationship in a different and unexpected way' (Caustonguay & Hill, 2012, p. 5).

To have a magical session, it is important to facilitate an emotional experience which encourages clients to take risks in doing things they may have previously avoided or not even considered. These moments in therapy can give clients a novel experience, which brings about more creativity and more positive emotions, while, at the same time, overriding old patterns and strengthening new ways of responding. More new information can be taken in by the client when the session embodies an element of surprise, fun, and curiosity (Armstrong, 2015). Having novel experiences in therapy may also increase the activity in the clients' neocortex region of the brain where problem-solving skills reside (Caspar & Berger, 2012). To facilitate the change process, therapists will need to be open to offering information and actions which are surprising and novel. As Rossi (2001) relates,

> Experiencing creative moments is the phenomenological correlate of a critical change in the molecular structure of proteins within the brain associated with the creation of new cell assemblies, memory and learning. Molecular transformation in the brain in response to psychological shock, arousal and novelty is now recognized by the author as the deep psychobiological basis of psychopathology as well as the educational, constructive and synthetic approach to healing and psychotherapy.
>
> *(p. 156)*

It is imperative that we view each client as a unique individual whose life experiences and personality are different from any other client. If we treat each client in the same manner, we lock ourselves into prearranged methods of responding, which will limit our ability to co-create an emotional experience that works for that particular client. Each client will need a different experience and a different approach. Therapists will need to be aware that, 'not all emotional experiences are the same, and different kinds of emotion reaction require different therapeutic interventions' (Elliot & Greenberg, 2007, p. 243). A therapeutic emotional experience for one client will be an energized, playful interaction, while another client will need a quiet, nurturing presence.

Essentially, in order to have a magical session, there needs to be a magical interaction. We have all witnessed, whether in person or on video, therapy performed in a deadly dull, scripted manner. We have also witnessed therapy performed with vibrancy. The difference in the sessions is the way in which the therapist interacts with the client. For a therapy session to be filled with wonder for clients, therapists will need to create a space for energy and vibrancy. It is in this kind of environment that clients connect with their own inner resources for healing. If therapists view themselves simply as outside observers to the therapy process, then they only can hope that the particular technique or theory that they are using will help the client change. But, as we previously discussed, research shows that there are actually no differences between client outcomes no matter what technique or theory is used.

Instead, it would be wise to view the therapist, not as an outside observer, but as a co-creator in the change process. Viewing the therapist as a helpful creator allows for more freedom in therapy because any change in the therapist can also bring about a change in the client. Therapists can no longer sit on the sidelines of therapy merely observing the action in the session. Instead, therapists should be actively engaged in an experiential performance that has the potential to be healing for the client. In spite of some theoretical orientations which say therapists and clients are locked into a predetermined narrative, actually, every moment of interaction between them provides an opportunity to offer something that is unique and life-changing.

For magic to happen in a session, therapists must feel free to discover their own unique method of conducting therapy. It is sometimes necessary for therapists to take unusual actions to help their clients to find a way out of their problems. When therapists offer novel and unusual experiences during the session, clients have an experience that alters limiting patterns of emotion and behavior. This type of interaction and the response from clients can create further opportunities for therapists to be even more creative as the session evolves. As Keeney (1983) states,

> The traditional view is that a therapist treats a client through a given intervention. However, it may be useful for a therapist to imagine a client's behavior as an intervention. His interventions, so to speak, attempt to provoke the therapist to come up with a useful directive or solution.

In this reverse view the therapeutic behavior is problematic when he fails to help the client. Treatment is successful when the client provokes the therapist to say or prescribe the appropriate action.

(p. 19)

When psychotherapy focuses on generating an emotional experience to help clients change, therapists cannot then rely strictly on theory to initiate the change process. One must become creative and inventive in working with each new client. Some clients will need intense and dramatic experiences in order to achieve their goals, while others may need a strong, quiet, and supportive interaction to make their breakthrough. Our personal ability to be flexible, to be who we are, or to be what is needed in that moment are assets in helping clients. As Nardone (1996) reminded us, 'The therapist is both the director and the principal actor of the movie. He or she must possess refined technical preparation, great methodological rigor, a lively creativity, and a great mental flexibility. In other words the therapist must simultaneously be a scientist and an artist' (p. 69).

We cannot underestimate the importance of an emotional interaction in therapy. Traditional healers have always valued the need for both the dramatic and the evocative. Krippner (2012) describes a time that he watched a healer in Trinidad. The healer, in addition, to supplying the clients with a variety of prayers and herbs, also used drama and performance. These actions, as well as the healer's gentle disposition, made the biggest impression. Krippner also found that healers from other parts of the world 'usually display a highly developed dramatic scene in carrying out healing rituals that enhance their power' (p. 74). This is not unlike the oral tradition of the Kalahari in Africa who believe that the stories that transform and heal them do so as a result of the impassioned and energetic qualities of the healer who tells them familiar stories (Keeney & Keeney, 2013b). As Laderman and Roseman (1996) found in their explorations of indigenous healers,

We cannot escape the idea that if healing is to be effective or successful, the senses must be engaged. Think of the belief common to many mystical philosophies that the way to the soul is through the senses. Is the way to health also through the senses? Are people simultaneously moved artistically, psychologically, and philosophically? Are there special connections

between particular kinds of aesthetic activity in the shaman's performance and the patient's experience of it?

(p. 4)

If the truth be told, much of modern psychotherapy appears lifeless compared with traditional approaches to healing. Indigenous healers performed ceremonies and dances and engaged the community in helping the afflicted person with the physical or emotional illness. Singing songs and conducting elaborate mystical rituals is very far removed from the world of psychotherapy today, where the presence of managed care and diagnostic labels hang in the air. The value of creativity has been replaced by a rigid adherence to evidence-based treatments, and the individual is lost in the complex web of the treatment. Keeney (2009) has suggested that it would be better to move psychotherapy out of the social sciences arena and, instead, move it into the area of the performing arts where creativity is encouraged.

Let us use an example of a usual therapy session that is being conducted with client and therapist sitting in the customary places and making routine comments. The session is going in the usual way until the client casually mentions that she likes music. What if the usual pattern of a therapy session was interrupted? What if the therapist asked the client to sing about her problem instead of talk about it? What if the therapist asked the client if the therapist could sing about the client's problem to her? What if the therapist asked the client what particular song comes to mind that reminds her of her problem? What if the therapist asked the client to write a song that gives her a solution to the problem? All of these possibilities open the door to a magical interaction. This excursion into a creative space moves therapy from an ordinary exchange into an unknown creative realm.

It is so important to reiterate that the emotional brain does not process information in the same way as our neocortex, which is analytic and logic oriented. The emotional brain, 'isn't really fazed by quiet, rational discussion, intellectual insight, or analytical arguments – some of the staples of modern psychotherapy' (Armstrong, 2015, p. xiv). The emotional brain responds more to sensory stimulation, symbols, metaphors, and unique experiences. Transformational therapy must incorporate both logic oriented and emotion-oriented applications. Providing clients with unique and uncommon experiences assists them to access their emotional brains. These experiences can help adjust the implicit meanings clients associate with their problems.

I once worked with a client, Marty, who was going through a big change in his life. His children were grown up and had moved out, and his wife had asked him for a divorce. Even though Marty was accepting of the divorce, this shook up his life, and he was having trouble adjusting to all the major changes happening to him. Marty had trouble concentrating at work; he had trouble sleeping, and overall, he showed signs of depression. He was an engineer who was very analytical in his thinking and was a natural problem solver, but he felt helpless because he couldn't solve his problems.

Our discussions in his first session centered mostly on his thoughts and feelings about the changes that were taking place. When discussing his cognitive patterns, it quickly became obvious to me that continuous exploration of his thoughts was not going to be very fruitful due to Marty's wonderfully engineer analytical mind. Marty was fully aware that he needed to manage his thoughts and he said that he saw his limiting beliefs about his situation and tried disputing them. The problem was, even though Marty's logical and rational mind was fully aware of the fact that life was going to change, his emotional brain was having trouble accepting that change. As a result, Marty was angry at himself for not being able to pull himself out of his funk and to move forward. He was stuck in his emotions, no matter what logical thoughts he attempted to think.

While we got to know each other in our first session, Marty said, in an offhand comment, that he enjoyed gardening, finding it to be both soothing and relaxing. For Marty, gardening was an escape from his world of stress. He discussed how he enjoyed digging in the dirt, planting new plants, and tending to the weeds in the flower beds in his backyard. Hearing about his love of gardening, I filed this nice piece of information away as I saw this hobby as a potential resource that Marty could use to move forward. Marty was attempting to tend the garden of his mind, but unfortunately, he could not keep the weeds of stress and grief at bay.

When Marty returned for his second session, he found that I had placed a tub of dirt with a trowel in the middle of the room. I gave Marty several sheets of white paper and asked him to write down in big letters every part of his present situation that he did not like. I then had Marty take the trowel and bury those papers in the dirt. Surprisingly, Marty did not ask me why he was doing this exercise. It was almost as if his emotional brain knew that he needed this activity because he quickly picked up the trowel and began digging deeply into the small pile of dirt. He placed the papers he had written on in the dirt and covered them up.

I then gave Marty several sheets of bright yellow paper on which he was to write his desired outcome for his new life. He was then directed to also bury these papers in the dirt. Once he was finished, I asked Marty to sit down and tell me about how he would like his garden at home to look over the next year. Marty gave me detailed answers about what plants he wanted to use and what the overall look of the garden would be. I then told Marty that if his life was a garden, he had begun a process at the beginning of our session to create the new garden of his life over the next year. I let him know that he could plant anything in it. Marty sat quietly and thought about what I had said.

At the end of the session, I asked Marty to choose which buried papers he wanted to cultivate and which ones he wanted to dig back up and discard. Marty was then directed to retrieve the papers he wanted to discard and burn them at home. He was to also take the tub of dirt with him and dump the dirt in a hole in his garden and plant something beautiful over it. Marty dutifully followed through on this directive and informed me at his next session that he had found that he was not quite as chained to his thinking as he had been. It seems that his emotional brain got the information that it could not find through logic and reason. The experience of digging in the dirt in a therapy session was much unexpected and out of the ordinary, an experience that Marty needed to connect with his own inner resources for planting new ideas in his mind for a new life.

By creating lively and emotional interactions with our clients, we indirectly connect with those indigenous healers who intuitively realized that the healing experience had to be different from everyday living. If one's experience in psychotherapy is no different from the conversations and engagements we usually have, then what is the point in seeking help? A session must be very different from a casual conversation with a friend or co-worker. It has to have that spark of wonder to activate our clients' emotional brains. It requires that we open up to being as creative as we can be as we navigate the unknown world clients bring to us. Kottler and Carlson (2009) remind us that, 'creativity is what is most novel and interesting, almost always generated out of uncertainty, ambiguity, and a position of creative indifference or not knowing' (p. 30).

Unleashing our creativity helps to expand our connections with our clients, deepens the levels of intimacy, and gives a solid foundation for new ideas to emerge in therapy. There has been recognition of how creativity can enhance collaboration between therapists and clients, since it encourages both parties to be flexible, to be adaptive, and to generate solutions (Carson & Becker, 2004). Essentially, creativity and psychotherapy complement each other. Rouse, Armstrong, and McLeod (2015) found that therapy and creativity have similar change processes. When they interviewed therapists who were also active artists, they found that both creativity and psychotherapy are relational processes. Both bring together diverse ways of experiencing, while also being a force for transformation and a source for professional identity. Having an openness to creativity has also been shown to support therapists' own abilities (Lawrence, Foster, & Tieso, 2015).

Becoming more creative in a session is not a skill that one can learn in a strict, linear fashion. It rather allows the unknown to emerge, something that one has never done before and in a completely different way. Creativity arises from the individual essence of the therapist and not through a scripted process, 'For creativity to realize its potential, it needs to become an approach, a way of viewing the processes of counseling, rather than just a series of techniques and interventions typed up and handed out in counselor education courses' (Lawrence et al., 2015, p. 171).

My dear friend and colleague, Dana Rideout, gave me a wonderful example of embracing creativity in order to access a client's emotional brain, and thereby making therapy magical. Not long after Dana moved into her own private practice, she had a new client named Kim. Kim had found her way to Dana after she already had several years of intensive psychotherapy. Kim began by immediately informing Dana that she had already been diagnosed with borderline personality disorder by her previous therapists. However, Kim had a good sense of humor and told Dana to 'not worry' about her previous diagnosis. Kim understood why most clinicians would bristle at that diagnosis since she had read much about borderline personality disorder. In fact, Kim had thoroughly investigated almost every aspect of her diagnostic label and had fully immersed herself in therapies purporting to effectively deal with border-line personality disorder. Kim believed this had helped her to be better equipped to navigate and manage her relationships. Unfortunately, it was a relationship struggle that brought Kim to Dana's office. However, it was not a relationship with a significant other or romantic partner, but rather it was the relationship she had with herself.

Kim was a fairly young woman and constantly had her hands full rearing three children, each from different fathers. She had dropped out of high school, but had returned to obtain her GED, and was attending classes at a local college. She was proud to have gone back to school, to have finished her GED, and to have obtained entrance into college. As much as she really loved school, unfortunately, Kim had to withdraw from her classes due to a severe mental health episode that had made attending school too difficult. For the last two years, she had worked at minimum wage jobs while she battled her emotional demons. Kim was a hard worker who did the best she could to provide for her children, but she believed she had limited options.

As Kim sat in Dana's office, she tearfully explained that the man presently living with her and her children, though not physically abu-sive, was emotionally abusive. He had a long history of seeking out sex-ual relations with other women while living off of her income. During the first part of her session, Kim described herself as 'broken,' 'unlov-able,' and 'stupid' for attracting the 'wrong' man. Kim struggled with a low self-image and her critical view of herself kept her away from social situations where people with education or status might be congregat-ing. She felt that she was being judged by others because of her frumpy appearance and her limited vocabulary.

While talking to Kim, Dana began to see that traditional talk ther-apy, which Kim had already participated in extensively, was eliciting the same victim language that kept Kim immobilized in her life. Dana also noticed that Kim had many positive resources that could be used in her therapy: her value of education, her work ethic, her resilience, and her sense of humor. Dana believed that if Kim could just have some sense of confidence, there would be a place in which to ground their therapy work. Kim had repeatedly said she wanted to feel better about herself, feel more empowered, talk with more authority, and stand with more self-efficacy; however, she believed she had never experienced these before and consequently wouldn't know if any of these goals were achieved.

On a creative whim, Dana asked Kim if she were willing to do something that she had never done previously. Kim was intrigued and said that she was willing. Dana told Kim that she needed to do something that was radically different from her other therapy and directed Kim to purchase two t-shirts on which she could write. She gave Kim no further explanation other than the directive to bring the shirts to the next session. When Kim arrived with her two t-shirts, Dana informed Kim that she was going to perform a special task designed just for her. On one t-shirt, with a fabric marker, Kim was directed to write, decorate, or draw anything that represented the critical self-talk in which she was currently engaging. Dana told her that any of the critical words, the heavy, edgy, self-deprecating labels and adjectives she routinely verbalized about herself needed to be written onto one of the t-shirts. Dana told Kim that if she chose to, she could use scissors, and even glue things to the shirts. In this task, Dana wanted Kim to have some freedom to create in her own way.

After she had finished the first shirt, Dana then directed Kim to sit quietly for a few moments. Then she was to illustrate on the second shirt how she really wanted to feel more in her life. She was asked to illustrate what she wanted her self-talk to sound like, what she wanted to express to others, and what she wanted to feel inside as she walked down a sidewalk or caught a reflection of herself in a store window. When she was given this project, Kim looked slightly worried since this was not the usual therapy she had experienced and lacked all the talk about problems. This assignment was out of the ordinary. In spite of her initial hesitancy, Kim was intrigued. Dana left her alone for a little while so that Kim could work on the project, but assured Kim that she would return toward the end of their session time to see what had been created.

When Dana reentered the therapy room, Kim had completed the project. Kim openly shared how difficult it had been for her to complete it. The first t-shirt she showed to Dana was a long-sleeved large green t-shirt that was, as Dana admitted, difficult to look at. The shirt was full of harsh, terrible words scrawled on the front and the back. Kim had even cut the sleeves and the bottom of the shirt to be excessively ragged. She had also cut a large hole in the center. Kim said she felt like nothing was in there, and therefore, it was just a big void. She said that this part of the project had really disturbed her because she had worked very hard during the last year to rebuild her life after receiving the borderline personality disorder diagnosis.

Then Kim showed Dana the second shirt, theoretically the more positive one. It was a long-sleeved bright orange t-shirt which she had not cut. It was clean. It was so clean that there was only one word written on the entire shirt. In the center of the shirt, Kim had simply drawn the letters 'o' and 'k.' She explained that she simply wanted to feel 'pure' as if the slate had been wiped clean, in the sense that she was 'ok.' Kim said that all she really wanted was to be grounded in 'ok.' Looking at the two different t-shirts, it was very apparent there was a discrepancy between what Kim wanted and how she presently felt.

Dana then asked Kim to follow her into the women's bathroom with her two t-shirts. With a large mirror in front of them, Dana asked Kim to slip on the cut up, critical green shirt. Kim was reluctant to put the shirt on. Dana, however, encouraged Kim to stand in front of the mirror with the green shirt on and to examine the emotions that came to her. Standing in front of the mirror with the cut up, critical green shirt with all of its holes and its negative words scribbled all over it. Kim began to cry. Kim's body really took on the emotional 'weight' of the critical green shirt. She said that the sadness she felt was akin to what a mother would feel for her child who had been bullied at school. Through her tears, Kim told Dana that she felt really sad that someone had to walk around feeling this way. At that point, Dana asked Kim to remove the green shirt and to explore the felt sense of peeling those words away from her body. Kim stood quietly for several moments while her mind and her body regained their equilibrium.

Kim did not fully realize the emotional weight of the green shirt until she pulled the second orange shirt over her head. After she straightened the orange shirt, she turned to look at herself in the mirror. In that moment, Kim stood straighter. Her gaze was softer, but at the same time more direct. Her breathing was much deeper and slower. Her posture was more comfortable. In all physical aspects, Kim really grew into 'ok' immediately. Both Kim and Dana felt a shift in the room. Something profound was happening to Kim and she started to cry again. This time, Kim explained she had no idea if she would ever get to 'ok,' but she said she had an inner knowing that she really wanted to get there. She said she liked the feeling of 'ok' immediately. She got it, she saw it, and she felt it. She now had her reference point. The moment was magical for her, something that she had not experienced in years of talk therapy.

From that moment on, any references to the choices Kim made in her self-talk, in her social interactions, and in all of her relationships were centered on the two t-shirts. Was Kim experiencing an 'orange' shirt event or a 'green' shirt event? She noted which of the two shirts drove most of her thoughts and behaviors between sessions. Kim reported that seeing her mirror reflection in the 'ok' shirt really gave her a sense of how to adjust her thinking to be more effective. Kim continued to keep both t-shirts and told Dana that having them close by helped her to measure her progress.

Over the following sessions, Kim continued to make remarkable progress. One day at the beginning of their session, Kim showed Dana with what she described as her new t-shirt. She informed Dana that it was an updated t-shirt. It was a clean white shirt filled with positive words, rainbows, sun rays, and lots of color. Kim smiled and said 'I think I've outgrown 'ok.' Dana's spirited interaction and activity helped to open the door for Kim's creativity and also allowed Kim to move beyond her self-limiting thoughts.

The free flow of moment to moment discourse between the therapist and the client is in itself a creative action. The open space of the exchange permits new information and action to emerge. Therapists have to use creativity in the redefining and reconstructing of the information that they receive from clients. People are always constructing different ways they experience their world. Because each person is constantly creating their own world, therapists cannot afford to exclude any consideration of creativity as they attempt to adjust these ways of experiencing life. If the duty of therapists is to move their clients out of their own limiting ways of experiencing their world in a creative manner, then therapists will need to use every ounce of creativity available to them to move clients out of their fixed, impoverished views of reality. Therapy is thus in itself a creative act which requires an engaging emotional experience.

INTUITION

As therapists navigate the ins and outs of a therapy session, there is often a reliance on two different approaches to the interaction: calculation and intuition. The bulk of what is taught in graduate school and continuing education training would be classified as the calculation category. Therapists in training spend much of their time learning theories, procedures, assessment, and techniques. They are taught to use good logic and reason to determine the best practices to use to help clients. This can be a very useful approach to working with cases.

However, in clinical research or discussion, there is not much time spent exploring intuition. Even though most professionals in the field would admit to using intuition as much or more than a calculated or trained response, there appears to be little encouragement or acceptance of the use of intuition in therapy. This may be because traditionally, intuition has been regarded as spiritual, spooky, or mystical, all of which can clash with the dominant view of decision making as being based on logic and reason. Due to its mysterious nature, intuition is indeed difficult to study. Since science is empirical and based on what can be observed and measured, intuition is a puzzling aspect of human experience which eludes a simple explanation. Intuition allows for decisions to be based on our own inner reflection and insights, and it can be a very quick way to connect patterns, which at the moment seem unconnected.

I contend that the role of intuition in therapeutic work has not been examined as much as it should have been in our clinical training. Intuition can be thought of as the spontaneous forming of impressions and the drawing of inferences in a nonconscious way of knowing. Almost every effective therapist I have ever met has talked about the importance of following 'clinical hunches' and 'gut feelings' in their work. Mars-Tarlow (2014b) contended that 'every psychotherapist relies on clinical intuition – whether in the form of flashbacks, hunches, gut feelings, body experiences, or behavioral impulses – to fill the gap between theory and practice. Clinical intuition is the means by which therapists perceive and respond to relational patterns during psychotherapy' (p. 392). Weis (2009) found that therapists who regularly utilize intuition in their work describe it as a blend of both the conscious and the unconscious observations which gives them a felt sense and a sensation of certainty and knowing. Welling (2005) states that, 'No therapist can reasonably deny following hunches, experiencing sudden insights, choosing directions without really knowing why, or having uncanny feelings that turn out to be of great importance for therapy' (p. 19).

Many therapists find intuition to be one of the most important tools in their work, and they come to rely on it. Jeffrey and Stone Fish (2011) found that many clinicians have a high regard for intuition and use it regularly in their work. These therapists viewed intuition as a unique source of information and direction. Laquercia (2005) states, 'Investigations of the subtle, often inexplicable, shifts in perception emanating from the depths of the psyche that often guide the analysts' responses rarely appear in the literature. And yet it is these unexpected and emotionally charged responses that frequently yield the most dramatic clinical results' (p. 68).

In the early days of psychotherapy, leading figures such as Sigmund Freud and Carl Jung noted the importance of using intuition in therapy. In the sometimes fast-paced, emotionally charged work that therapists deal with, there is a great benefit in utilizing the rapid nature of intuition. Laub (2006) states that there are many different ways in which intuition can appear in clinical work. Laub found evidence for the use of intuition in such areas as metaphors, dreams, symbolism, and nonverbal communication. Other researchers have found that the use of intuition can be very effective, but only if there is ample trust between the client and the therapist, as well as the clinician's trust in his or her own gut feelings. Bohart (1999) believes that intuition is really inspiration that just spontaneously occurs to the therapist while in the flow of the therapeutic interaction. It appears that the topic of intuition needs more exploration since it may help our clients within the therapeutic relationship.

From an evolutionary development view, clinical intuition has been seen as connected 'with the automatic operation of the parental instinct as hard-wired into the human brain within the limbic, emotional/motivational circuitry shared by all minds' (Marks-Tarlow, 2014a, p. 147). Intuition has also been described in terms of an embodied experience which gives one the sensation of having a 'gut feeling' (Tantia, 2014). Alternatively, intuition has been regarded as coming from therapists' own experiences and schemas rather than from an outside base of knowledge (Bohart, 1999). Others simply believe intuition is one's ability to sense connections at the unconscious level. It is through the use of intuition that therapists are able to 'detect and respond to relational patterns both within our patients and within ourselves. In order to perceive patterns within a healing context, clinicians need to know, and just as importantly to feel, the minds of others. Sometimes the melding of minds takes on rather extraordinary dimensions' (Marks-Tarlow, 2012, p. 21).

This implicit way of knowing gives us the ability to feel that something is not quite as it appears, even in spite of logical evidence that it is. Even though our rational minds may see no connection between two totally different things, it is our intuitive side which tells us that there is more to the story than what we may logically think. Since intuition plays such an important part in clinical work, it is reasonable to ask why there is little discussion of this phenomenon in psychotherapy training. The answer may be that many professionals in the field of psychotherapy want their work completely rooted in empiricism in order to be regarded as a science rather than an art. Intuition may be viewed as too connected to spirituality and mystical leanings rather than aligned within 'hard science.' The lack of operational definitions and applications can make it problematic for researchers who investigate intuition in order to quantify its operation.

Intuitive insights just seem to come to us out of nowhere, and the insights that appear to us also have an accompanying feeling that something important is about to emerge. The information that we receive comes from a place that is far removed from our conscious thinking. It is when we open ourselves to the feelings or images which emerge and then apply our conscious thought to these feelings and images that magical clinical insight springs forth. Therapists obtain information from the environment due to the nature of the interaction between themselves and clients. It is in the back and forth flow of a conversation that is not burdened by excessive structure that permits therapists to recognize patterns and connections at the unconscious level. If our sessions are too regimented, we inhibit the flow of this potentially valuable information and patterns. This awareness and use of intuitive insights can lead us to make seemingly magical connections that can be shocking. Preoccupation with structure which restrains creative interaction will block our intuition from gaining access to the necessary information our clients need for healing.

It is important to trust ourselves and allow ourselves to be open to intuition. Awareness of the sensations that we feel and the images we perceive from unconscious origins can lead to new insights which could alter the course of therapy. We can give permission to ourselves to follow the path to intuition. This may be scary to some therapists because of fears that sharing the intuitive information will appear odd or totally unrelated to what is taking place in the session and could cause a disruption in the rapport with our clients.

Since the prevalent approach to the clinical arena continues to be directed by empiricism and standardization of treatments, there is little space left for teaching therapists to trust themselves (and their intuition) more often. The employment of regimented therapeutic techniques often limits a practitioner's access to important internal wisdom. The 'cookie cutter' approach to therapy leaves few openings for investigating our clinical hunches. Perhaps there is a middle ground that not only gives therapists a structure in which to work, but also honor the mystery of our unconscious intelligence? I think there is, and most therapists, who routinely follow their 'gut feelings' in the therapy room, would probably concur.

A magical session incorporates the use of therapist intuition because intuition leads us to places where we did not expect to travel. It guides us to an awareness that there is more in the moment than we may consciously think. Using our intuition may involve our introducing odd statements and adding odd actions in the therapy discourse. What may not seem to make sense initially, may connect in ways we do not at first comprehend. Allowing these odd changes in direction can release the therapy session from predictable meanderings. The use of intuition can also give us tools to move clients out of their habitual ways of responding to their problems. We would be wise to remember that, 'Within psychotherapy, intuition and imagination go hand in hand' (Marks-Tarlow, 2012, p. 152).

I was once working with a young woman, named Heidi, who was in recovery from a methamphetamine addiction. Heidi was trying to get her life back together and also heal the pain that her addiction had caused. She did not feel good about herself because of her history of drug use and she constantly worried about falling back into her dysfunctional patterns. Our topic of conversation on that particular day was her learning how to soothe herself when she became distraught instead of her automatically turning to unhealthy actions. Heidi admitted that she was often uncomfortable with her own emotions and was tempted to turn to less than resourceful distractions to avoid feeling uncomfortable.

Suddenly, a strong image popped into my mind. I found that I was seeing a vivid picture of a large number of flying birds. This image made absolutely no sense to me, and I initially chose to dismiss it from my mind. Yet, for some reason, I felt compelled to trust this intuitive flash.

In spite of my concerns about the nonsensical nature of the image and about the possible disruption in the flow of our interaction, I asked Heidi what 'birds' meant to her. She stopped for a second and then clarified my question, 'Are you asking me what birds mean to me? Like, what they stand for to me?' I nodded my head in approval of her appraisal of my question.

Heidi paused for a few moments and sat with a puzzled look on her face. She then told me that what came to her mind was a memory of when she was a young girl. Heidi and her grandmother would feed the birds that gathered in her grandmother's large backyard. The two of them would go outside and sit in two chairs in the shade of a tree on a hot summer's day and throw out breadcrumbs for the birds to eat. The birds would fly down to retrieve the crumbs and both grandmother and granddaughter delighted in seeing the birds come so close. Heidi told me that it was a special time for her and she still missed seeing her grandmother who had died many years ago.

As Heidi talked about this time period, tears came to her eyes. She explained that the times she spent with her grandmother were the few occasions in her life when she felt that she was 'safe and good.' Sitting quietly and feeding the birds was a connective experience for her. It was obvious that she missed her grandmother, and I wondered if this could be a soothing experience she could use in the future. I asked Heidi if she were open to feeding the ducks who gathered at a pond across the street from my office. With a big smile, she quickly agreed. We walked over to the pond and she watched the ducks for a while. I showed her a bench so that she could sit comfortably the next time that she came with food for the ducks. Heidi appeared to enjoy this moment and seemed profoundly touched by our excursion to the pond.

In time, Heidi found that she was able to reconnect with the feeling that she had with her grandmother when she fed the ducks. She also decided that she would feed the ducks anytime she felt overwhelmed by life and needed to soothe herself. Heidi now had another experience she could call upon when she was feeling stressed. The intuitive image my mind gave me, initially totally unrelated to our work, gave Heidi a positive resource to use for her healing, and experience with which she had previously lost touch.

Having the courage to take what our intuition gives us and run with it is necessary to reap therapeutic rewards. Just because an idea or an image may appear strange to us is not reason enough to discontent its usefulness for our clients. My colleague, Bette Freedson, is a very effective clinician who routinely allows herself to follow her intuition. She feels her use of intuition is a core aspect of her effectiveness as a therapist. She related to me a case she was working with a man whom we will call Jay. It was their first session and she had not previously met him. Jay was feeling depressed and anxious due to his deliberating about leaving his marriage. He was also grappling with the idea of returning to his home state to be with a woman with whom he had secretly begun a relationship.

Jay told Bette how he had moved to his present location after marrying his wife. His friends and family had told him that moving to be with his new wife would be a huge mistake. They informed him that he would deeply regret his decision and things would not turn out well for him. At the time, Jay had ignored his friends and family's concerns, but now, he began to believe they had been right. Jay felt helpless to do much different in his present life. He was very unhappy in his marriage, but he was very hesitant to do anything different as he was terrified that he would make another 'mistake.' This fear overwhelmed him and held him paralyzed. Jay felt he could not make a decision as to what to do. He felt he was stuck and could not determine if he should stay or if he should go.

As Bette was listening to Jay talk about his dilemma, she had a flash of intuition. In her mind she had a vision of a village of indigenous people who had a sorcerer who dealt out curses to those who violated certain codes of conduct set down by the village. Bette informed Jay that she could not tell him what to do. She told him that she realized he was in a tough situation. She decided to share her intuitive vision with Jay.

Bette told Jay that, with his situation, if he had been a part of an indigenous group who believed in hexes, then she would say he had been hexed. Jay suddenly sat up straight and appeared more focused on what Bette was saying. Bette told him that hexes can work, but only if the person creating the hex and particularly the person who is the victim of the hex both strongly believed that the hex will work. She reiterated that the person who believes they are hexed will often manifest the symptoms of the hex.

Jay was now fully absorbed in what Bette was saying and told her that her comment made perfect sense to him. His mood appeared to brighten upon hearing Bette's thoughts about hexing. Bette informed Jay that he could begin the process of removing his hex by freeing himself from the belief that he had made a mistake just because his present situation had not worked out as he had hoped. She told Jay that to better protect himself from believing in the 'hex,' they could discuss how much he had learned about himself and how much he had grown as a person as a result of moving to be with his wife. Jay seemed to be relieved at the thought he could remove his hex and made another appointment with Bette to discuss further ways he could free himself from the debilitating negative belief. In fact, when Jay came to his second session, he was open to acknowledging how much his decision to marry and move had taught him about life. Bette's willingness to use what her intuitive mind gave her ultimately resulted in Jay feeling more grounded and more motivated to make the changes he wanted to make in his therapy sessions.

IMPROVISATION

To open up a space for magic to appear, a therapist will need to become comfortable with improvisation. When one is improvising, he or she is spontaneously performing without preplanning or preparation. One's actions are unrehearsed and unscripted. The aliveness of the present moment is embraced without referring to strict pre-planned criteria of how one should act. The therapist who embraces improvisation allows for unique and inspired interactions to occur which can rejuvenate sessions that may have become stale or staged.

In her groundbreaking book, 'Improvisation for the Theater,' famed director and acting coach Viola Spolin (1999) defined improvisation as a process in which one is 'setting out to solve a problem with no preconception as to how you will do, permitting everything in the environment (animate or inanimate) to work for you in solving the problem' (p. 361). I believe that this definition is one that should be taken to heart by psychotherapists. When we are working with our clients, we need to be open to the moment to moment interaction without having any rigid preconceptions of how we will help our clients. If we allow what will come to be as it is, without caging our clients in prearranged scenarios, openings to move clients toward their own solutions can appear in ways that we could never have imagined. Gergen (2009) states that for action-oriented therapists, 'Much would be gained by collaborating with specialists in improvisation training. ... In a world of complex relationships and mercurial fluctuations in meaning, we must increasingly rely on improvisation for effective co-action' (p. 309).

Improvisation in the therapy room allows both the therapist and the client to connect with each other's authentic way of being in that moment. By offering each other space to be authentic, trust is generated and maintained. The interaction becomes more valuable and animated as each participants' unique perceptions and reactions are honored and encouraged. Spontaneity in a session encourages clients to 'get out of their heads' and release the desire of determining what will happen in the next moment (Farley, 2017). An improvisational interaction also encourages clients to move beyond their preconceived stuck points and to expand their imaginations about what is indeed possible (Galvez & Crouch, 2017; Keeney, 2009; Kindler & Gray, 2010; Knoblauch, 2001; Ringstrom, 2011; Romanelli, Tishby, & Moran, 2017).

Often, clients have difficulty adjusting to change in their lives because of their rigid set of cognitive, emotive, and behavioral patterns. In attempting to deal with new changes in life and with the unknown, clients will generally continue to use patterns of interaction which are familiar to them. As Montuori (2003) asserts, 'A defining quality of creative improvisation is precisely the generation of the unpredictable, the unusual, the unforeseen' (p. 239). A session that allows therapist and client to experience spontaneity can also help clients become open to new ways of dealing with challenges. Having a playful attitude regarding the unknown goes a long way in generating more resiliency in life changes.

Improvisation can also be a means for therapists to become more effective in their work and in how they interact with their clients. The use of improvisation in clinical training has been shown to be helpful in lowering anxiety, expanding empathic listening, and increasing self-awareness for therapists in training. Being in the moment and relinquishing the desire to control a situation helps one become more comfortable and more accepting of whatever emerges. Learning to allow for changes in direction aids in increasing flexibility with interactions. Since one cannot predict what will happen, remember that anything that occurs can be used to further therapy. Improvisation has also been found helpful in becoming more comfortable with appropriate risk taking and dealing effectively with ambiguity (Lawrence et al., 2015).

Therapists who operate in an improvisational mode create openings for change. Improvising offers therapists and clients a pathway that moves beyond habitual responses in ways of responding and toward novel experiences. All parties involved can appreciate the present moment as they indirectly give each other permission to be less than perfect and to take risks. This opens up access to client resources from which clients can pull from when dealing with their problems. Since there is no fixed script, the therapy session can benefit from the unknown, and the roles each 'performer' plays can abruptly change into something more enchanting and exciting. The co-creation of the present moment by therapist and client can yield many new opportunities for transformation that a fixed theoretical agenda might perhaps impede (Ringstrom, 2003).

For therapists to successfully suspend any preparation for a session, they have to be willing to let go of their own preconceptions and judgments about what therapy should look like. They must be open to discovering something new and be able to flow with each moment. Stopping the free flow of creative interaction in therapy in order to follow a scripted technique does much to hamper progress. It is in these moments of inventive, original interaction that clients' paradigms can be expanded. As Pagano (2012) observed, 'the therapist's use of self in playful improvisation is a critical and necessary vehicle for change on growth in the patient' (p. 205).

Often, therapists are afraid to let go of prearranged frameworks in therapy. Perhaps sitting right in the middle of the great creative unknown causes them anxiety as anything could happen. Clinging to safety with scripted responses does little to inspire clients or to expand one's abilities as a therapist. Most clients know when their therapists are genuinely with them in the moment or if they are only silently checking off criteria in their minds. Being spontaneous and fully in the moment in a session is helpful since it is necessary to work with what emerges as soon as it arrives. As Farley states (2017), 'in clinical work, spontaneity is the core meta-counseling skill. We never know who and/or what will present from session to session and we need to be able to be in the here-and-now so that we can spontaneously respond to whatever emerges with our clients' (p. 120).

If improvisation is allowed into the therapeutic interaction, both clients and therapists can co-create a new way for clients to relate to their problems. Improvisation in therapy 'is effective because it represents a shift in the therapist's mode of being, and as such, activates a parallel shift in the patient' (Pagano, 2012, p. 206). The magical element of creativity shines through when there is an interaction of spontaneity between the two parties. When this creativity is not only allowed, but fully embraced, both clients and therapists can be transformed since both have been part of the creation. Therapists are free to create their own particular style which is found in the dynamic improvisational exchange with their clients.

I remember working with a new therapist who, in spite of her desire to be a good therapist, found herself stuck in what I call 'cookie cutter methods' of therapy. She followed all the techniques to the letter and said all the right things, but she reported to me that she was having trouble implementing her skills. I agreed to sit in on one of her sessions to observe and then to give her feedback. I applauded her desire to seek feedback to improve her skill.

The client whose session I sat in on was an older woman, whom I will call Brenda, who was having problems with anxiety. Brenda had trouble staying focused on her daily tasks and had been worrying excessively about her adult children who lived in another state. Brenda was very pleasant and had no issue with my sitting in on the session. It appeared that she really wanted to be an active participant in the therapy process, and part of me wished that I could have a client as nice and as motivated as she was.

Once the session began, the therapist asked Brenda how she was feeling at that moment. Brenda replied that she was feeling a little anxious because earlier in the day she left a message on her son's voicemail and he had not yet responded. Even though she knew that he was working and probably very busy, she still worried that something bad might have happened to him. The therapist then told Brenda that it was time for them to go over the breathing exercises they had talked about in the last session. The therapist then pulled out a sheet of paper from which she read the directions to the woman. The therapist then coached Brenda through a process she was to use to monitor her breathing. This was supposed to help her to relax.

At the end of the process, the therapist asked Brenda how she felt. Brenda said she was slightly better, but she was still very worried about her son. At this point, the therapist pulled out another sheet of paper and told Brenda that they were now going to take an inventory of Brenda's cognitive distortions. They diligently went through the whole process. At the end when asked how she was feeling, Brenda again replied she was a little better, but she was still worried about her son. At this point, the therapist started to pull out another sheet of paper. I could take no more.

'What message did you leave on your son's voicemail?' I asked Brenda. She seemed surprised that I spoke up (as did the therapist). 'I just told him I was thinking about him and asked if he would call me if he got a chance.' 'Hmmm,' I wondered aloud. 'That doesn't sound like a very fun message to me.' Brenda looked a little perplexed by my comment. 'How do you mean?' she asked. 'I just mean that if you really want to grab his attention, then you may need to leave a more creative message than that.' 'How so?' Brenda asked with a slight smile. The therapist then spoke up and said, 'I don't think the message is the problem here, but rather her ...' I immediately cut her off as I focused on Brenda. 'I am just saying that a message that just says call me when you can is not really geared to make anyone curious enough to call you. Why not make a really creative, out of the ordinary call and see how much faster he calls you back?'

'I'm sorry, but I really don't see how ...' the therapist began as she tried to pull our conversation back to Brenda's anxiety before I waved her away. 'How about calling your son and telling him that he just won a special award that entitles him to call his mother? Or maybe call him as if you were his mother's personal assistant who is interested in setting a scheduled talk? You could use a funny name on that one!' I grinned at Brenda, who clearly was confused but also intrigued at my spontaneous interruptions of the session and of her anxiety. 'I don't know if I could do that.' Brenda said as she started to grin. 'Why not? It might give him a laugh and make him call back sooner. Let's come up with a way to mess with your son in a fun way and then you can call him while you are in here with us. We can listen in as you record your message. That would be fun!' I was throwing out something off the wall to see how she would react.

My 'out of the blue' improvisation about the phone call seemed to really click with Brenda. She and I came up with a silly way to call her son in which she said that she was not really sure that she would be available for his next phone call. This was due to her very busy schedule the next day of dining with the Queen of England, playing polo with members of the United States Congress, and having a fashion show that was to showcase her latest designs. The therapist had given up saying anything else as Brenda and I ignored each comment she made about returning to the topic of anxiety. Brenda made her call in the office on her cell phone as we listened in on her comedic message. She played it up and adopted an English accent and regaled her son with all the things that she was doing tomorrow and then apologized for the possibility that she might not answer his call. When she hung up the phone, we were all laughing at her wonderful performance.

I asked Brenda when was the last time that she had enjoyed being silly as she had been in her message to her son. She replied that she was not having much fun in her life as of late. I told her that perhaps her worry about her children might actually be energy built up and not properly used for fun. The phone message performance led into a discussion about how she could be having more fun in her life. Having more fun meant less anxiety and she was open to exploring the new theme in therapy of pursuing fun.

As we were wrapping up the session, Brenda's phone rang. It was her son who was laughing as she said hello. He said that she had made his day with her silly message. Improvising on the theme of the phone message moved the therapy session out of the theme of client deficit and into the theme of seeking more fun. The session became more lively and interactive. The therapist's rigid adherence to a scripted approach with clients was why she was not getting the results she sought. To her credit, she decided to let loose and only refer to her sheets some of the time.

There is little to no preparation needed in order to successfully improvise in a session. When a therapist attempts to coerce a specific action, then the potential for a positive shift in the interaction becomes limited. Permitting the session to move where it will, allows the participants to become active creators of new outcomes. The challenge for therapists is to stay present and open as the course of therapy moves into unknown places, which is crucial for magical moments to appear. Therapists and clients who allow a space for imagination, perceive their work together as creative, and this can lead to new understandings and new ways of relating (Ringstrom, 2008).

Clients seek help from a therapist because they feel 'stuck' in some manner. Their ability to work through the perceived problem is often hindered by their attempting to deal with the problem with a pattern of action/reaction which further cements the problem and, unfortunately, makes it worse. If clients cling to the same patterns of action, thought, and emotion, then the problem will be maintained. Clients will then feel the problem is insurmountable and cannot be overcome. This will lead to the perception of the problem as their personal reality and their automatic response to this 'reality' further solidifies the pattern.

In order to facilitate a change in these patterns, therapists will need to be comfortable with improvisational activities that are unexpected and appear random to clients. When new and random information enters their perceived reality, then their reality has to readjust. As previously stated, straightforward logical information in dialogue may not always be effective since the brain is 'stuck' in a deeply entrenched pattern. Introducing the random into a session can cause the brain to experience different and new realities, thus creating a shift in how clients respond to their problems.

Random information can come from almost anywhere, but it does not come from rehearsed treatment protocols. It can only come from an alive interaction with much room for spontaneity. It also does not come from excessive problem investigation. When we allow the random to show up in our therapy room, we can first expect that many of the interventions will appear absurd to our clients. However, this should not discount the therapeutic effectiveness of absurdity since it helps clients to have new experiences which might otherwise be dismissed by their overly analytical minds.

Odd, unexpected, and absurd actions in psychotherapy are not what one usually learns in graduate school. In fact, in my many years in training, giving absurd directives was never covered. There were examples of founding leaders in the field who sometimes did strange things to create change, but this idea was never followed up with encouragement or explanations on how to take such actions. In examining the use of the random and absurdity in therapy, it is the unexpected that creates a sense of confusion in clients thereby opening space for new possibilities to emerge.

Even though great therapists such as Whitaker, Haley, Erickson, Palazzoli, and so on, have used the random and the absurd in their work, there is not much information in the research about how to or why to perform such maneuvers. Being open to randomness and absurdity not only makes one a more flexible therapist, but absurdity can shake up interactions so that clients are forced to find a new and different way of relating to the situation which brought them to therapy.

In order to create magic in the therapy room, clinicians must be 100 percent willing to abandon rigid ways of interacting with clients. They must be prepared to act in an improvisational and creative manner. Essentially, *to be absurd is to not make any sense.* This statement will clash with the prevailing paradigm of logical, left-brained therapy which appears to engulf much of the evidence-based research. Therapists are routinely told that they need to teach their clients to think and act rationally in order for them to change. Certainly, these can be worthwhile objectives, but I raise the point that it is in learning to deal with the absurdity of life that we really learn to become more flexible. When we become confused, we naturally search for understanding. While we are trying to make sense of absurd actions, we automatically are stretched out of our habitual ways of relating to our world. From this stretching process, we become more resourceful in how we respond to the absurdity of the moment and to life in general.

I once saw a couple who were having issues due to the wife's unwillingness to let her husband have any power in their relationship. Even though she was very controlling, at the same time, she wanted her husband to 'step up' and take some control in their household. The husband really wanted to do this, but every time he attempted to 'step up,' she would start a fight with him because it triggered her own control issues. He would back down from seeking to take any further form of control to maintain harmony in the relationship. The husband was stuck in a double bind situation. Even though both the husband and the wife logically knew what the situation was, nothing was changing. They felt trapped in these reactive patterns and helpless to change them. They had sought couples therapy from another therapist, but they had found it difficult to follow the directives given by their previous therapist because their relational patterns were so entrenched.

After listening to the couple's complaints in the first session and hearing how their previous therapy directives were ineffective, I knew that any form of talk therapy would probably not work for their situation. Instead, I told them that they were a very special couple, and this was a very special case. I informed them that no ordinary intervention would work with a couple such as themselves. However, I had a unique plan that I wanted them to follow. I let them know that I had never given this unique plan to any other couple I had worked with in the past (if the truth be known, I just let my improvisational nature flow and came up with the idea on the spot). Once I had thoroughly piqued their interest, I obtained their agreement to do anything that I asked them to do as long as it did not violate any safety, security, or ethical boundaries. They agreed to my terms. I then excused myself from the room for a moment in order to build their curiosity.

When I walked back into the room, I found them sitting slightly closer together, probably discussing their anticipation about what I was going to say. I looked at both of them intently and then said, 'As I previously said, you two are a unique couple. I am not going to waste your time with any surface, shallow therapy. I truly believe that the two of you require something radically different to begin your work with me. You have shown yourselves to be very motivated and you have given me your word that you would do what I asked, and I respect how committed you are to your relationship to make that agreement.' I paused for a moment to build the anticipation a little more. 'Now, I want you to do something a little different. I know that you want things to be different at home, right?' I asked them. They nodded in the affirmative.

'Good' I said. 'I want you both to go home, and on the next day that you are both home alone with nowhere to go, I want you to wear each other's clothing for the whole day.' They both looked shocked. I pointed to the husband and said, 'You are to wear one of your wife's dresses,' and then pointing to the wife I said, 'And you are to wear one of his business suits. You both are free to do whatever you want to do that day, but you are not allowed to talk about how you feel about the change of clothing.' There was a brief silence in the room as the couple looked at me and then at each other.

'That is kind of crazy, isn't it?' said the husband. 'Yes' I replied. 'But so is the dysfunctional pattern both of you are locked in.' 'He won't fit into anything other than my nightgown,' said the wife in a concerned tone. 'Then a nightgown it is,' I replied. They both appeared unsure of how to take what I had just given them. They reluctantly agreed and said that they could do this 'change of clothes activity' the next day. I dismissed them from the session quickly to avoid any last-minute change of heart regarding this absurd therapy directive.

At their next session, two weeks later, the couple told me that they had followed the directive even though they felt very uncomfortable and silly doing so. The husband spent the entire day walking around the house in his wife's nightgown, even doing some woodwork in the garage with it on. The wife said that she had worn his gray business suit with one of his ties. Although it almost swallowed her since her husband is much larger than she. Both told me that the whole day had felt off-kilter and they were relieved to be able to return to their own wardrobe choices the next day.

However, the couple also told me about a curious turn of events which started over the next few days after their clothing exchange. The wife had begun to allow the husband to take on more responsibility in the home. She found that she did not feel the same need to micromanage his efforts. She still had a long way to go, but she said that she was giving him a little more freedom to 'step up' and do things. The husband found himself more willing to take advantage of her offer and had started taking over more activities. There were still problems with their control patterns, but the absurdity of the task I had given them had apparently shaken up some of their usual ways of responding to each other.

In order to effectively use absurd actions in therapy, we need to be sure that we have our clients' best interests at heart and that we ask them to do only that which we are willing to do ourselves. We are creating an alive 'Zen Koan' in the therapy room when we allow absurdity in. By being open to improvisation, we free ourselves to be more creative in our interventions. There is no fixed pattern when we are operating out of a frame of improvisation. Improvising gives therapists and clients the freedom to do and become whatever is needed in order to bring about change.

UTILIZATION

If I had to pick one idea that was most important for creating an alive, improvisational therapy session, I would probably choose the concept of utilization. This concept finds its roots in the magical work of the psychiatrist Milton H. Erickson. Erickson was renowned for his effective, magical, and, at times, bizarre interventions with clients. Erickson was a practitioner who appeared to have no specific agenda for working with clients because his interventions appeared to be based on what the client presented in the session, rather than on any predetermined therapeutic maneuvering. He was adept at assimilating any part of his clients' actions or life experiences into the direction of therapy in order to facilitate the client's growth.

Often therapists have certain prerequisites for how therapy should progress in order for it to be successful. When utilization is applied in a therapy session, there are no preset conditions that need to be satisfied for therapy to progress. Behaviors, which initially may appear to block the unfolding of the therapeutic process, can be used to advance the obtaining of therapeutic goals. Any potential action on the part of clients is viewed as helpful in assisting those clients in accessing their own individual resources in order to make powerful changes in their lives. Instead of battling any actions that clients make which we may perceive as resistant, utilization allows therapists to use the clients' defensive defiance or refusal to move them toward a place where those same actions can be of benefit to the course of therapy.

Utilization is an approach which accepts that our clients have a right to behave in a resistant way. We then organize situations based upon clients' responses in a manner that benefits those clients. Utilization can be thought of as 'a perspective of optimism and confidence in the clients' ability to respond to treatment' (Dolan, 1985, p. 7). Rather than label client's resistant action as character flaws, Erickson would 'take it upon himself to learn the individual's pattern of behavior and response. He would then utilize these patterns in service of change, rather than treating them as blocks' (O'Hanlon, 1987, p. 10). Erickson's concept of utilization views any client's cognition, emotion, or behavior as having the possibility to initiate change. Countering resistance with a nonjudgmental attitude, the therapist can allow any action on the part of the client to be of benefit to the interaction.

Put simply, utilization is accepting and validating whatever clients may bring into the therapy room. Even if what is brought by the client may be initially considered dysfunctional, utilization grants the therapist the ability to build upon client actions and to channel clients' experiences into a more resourceful outcome. By flowing with their clients' patterns and adjusting their approach, therapists have the ability to create an opening to move clients toward different patterns of behavior. Utilization aids in maintaining the crucial therapeutic alliance because there is no fighting for dominance between therapist and client. This can lead to more collaborative work toward therapeutic goals, instead of division and struggle. When clients' responses are taken and utilized in a way to move therapy forward, clients will experience a difference in how someone responds to them which may have previously been negative or adversarial. This helps clients feel validated and accepted, which contributes to an effective working relationship.

It is natural to encounter resistance on the part of clients. Often, this is due to clients coming to identify their own sense of self with their problem. Resistance appears when therapists attempt to change the problem without fully understanding that, at some level, clients feel that a change in the problem will be a change in their identity. Any change in who we think we are can feel strange and scary, so it is natural that clients may sometimes resist positive change. Clients may choose to continue harmful patterns rather than to experience a dramatic restructuring of their sense of self. Utilization helps therapists avoid clashes with clients over change. Therapists do not directly force clients to be different from what they think they are.

In one of Erickson's most cited examples of utilization, he once worked with a patient in the hospital who believed he was Jesus Christ. The male patient was well known at the hospital for creating disturbances on his ward due to his aggressive preaching and proselytizing. He saw himself as the Messiah and attempted to spiritually save everyone on his ward. The man's actions led to his being restrained and isolated for long periods of time. Apparently, nothing appeared to work to cause the patient to change his behavior or his delusional belief that he was Jesus Christ.

When Erickson became the primary psychiatrist on the ward, he decided he would not argue or fight with the patient about his identity. He simply utilized what the patient was already doing. One day, Erickson approached the man and asked if he were really Jesus Christ. The patient replied in the affirmative. At that point, Erickson then asked the man if he would do him a favor. Erickson told the man that since he was indeed really Jesus Christ Erickson could use his help. Erickson explained that since the patient was Jesus Christ, he knew the patient must have been a carpenter. The patient replied that he indeed had been a carpenter. Erickson then asked for the patient for his help with building a bookcase. The man agreed to help Erickson.

This started the process of directing the patient toward better interactions with the staff and fellow patients, more productive work, and a sense of accomplishment. In time, the patient significantly improved. By utilizing the patient's behavior, no matter how bizarre, toward an effective goal, Erickson was able to make tremendous progress where other approaches had dismally failed (Haley, 1973).

For a magical session to take place, therapists need to work toward being in a state of openness to be able to respond to whatever comes forth in the session. If clients feel we are trying to block them or manipulate them in any way, they will naturally resist therapy directives and will become noncompliant to treatment goals. For therapy to be effective, the therapists' ability to guide clients toward positive outcomes needs to be a co-creative process instead of a contest for who will win. Utilization helps maintain the flow and interaction of therapy, while building connection and direction toward a mutually agreed upon result. As Mitchell (2012) relates,

> In order to avoid the pitfalls of typical responses and the resistance that follows, you must consistently strive to avoid the commonplace. You must avoid typical verbal and non-verbal responses. In doing this, you surprise clients, you confound their anticipation of your response, and you begin disrupting the patterns that are inherent to their problems.
>
> *(p. 38)*

I once worked with a client named Cindy who had the annoying habit of pointing out all the reasons why any situation or task would not work well. Cindy was permanently focused on what was wrong with things and with why things might not work. She was a pleasant person, but her natural tendency to tear ideas apart looking for the reasons why they would not work was becoming tiring in our sessions. It did not matter what suggestion or directive I offered, Cindy let me know in no uncertain terms why my ideas would not work, and if they should work, how they could have been better.

After fully realizing that this pattern of behavior was blocking any success in obtaining our therapy goals, I decided that, rather than fighting it, I would utilize this pattern. In our next session, as usual, Cindy began her pattern of informing me of why any intervention I suggested would not work. I listened intently to her and then I thanked her. I told her that her ability to see the long-term outcome was a gift and I appreciated her sharing her insights with me. I told her that I was impressed that she was comfortable enough in the therapeutic relationship to be so open and direct.

I then asked Cindy if she had ever thought about using her unique ability to spot potential issues into some employable skill. She was evidently surprised that I was no longer fighting with her. She told me that she was unsure what I meant. I then told her that many businesses hire consultants to tear apart business plans and business projections so that they can be sure to effectively deal with potential problems. Many of these consultants made a great deal of money for their insight. I asked Cindy if she would continue using this unique skill in our sessions. I told her that it really helped me to note any potential problems with my ideas which I might not have previously considered. I also asked her to help me to formulate better plans so that our work together could be successful.

Cindy was slightly taken aback by my request for her to take the very actions which annoyed so many other people in her life. She was accustomed to arguing with people about her assertions which created hurt feelings between herself and others. My request went counter to the responses that she had received throughout her life. From that point on, even though Cindy still countered any idea I had, she also came with her own idea of how we could make my idea better. Thus began our process of truly co-creating the outcomes she wanted to achieve in her life. In time, Cindy also began to entertain the idea of going back to school to major in business so that she could one day become one of those highly paid consultants who were valued for their challenges to others' ideas.

Utilization does not have to only involve client resistance. Any positive action on the part of clients can be utilized to help them change. If a client has a sense of humor, it can be utilized to move the session in a more effective direction. If a client informs the therapist that she has natural artistic ability, this also could be used to build resources. Whatever springs forth from the interaction can be used to facilitate change.

A major element of creating a magical session involves nurturing an environment of surprise and curiosity while promoting intuitive knowing, improvisational action, and the utilization of client responses. When these conditions are in play, therapy takes a turn toward something more than a professional conversation about change. It becomes unique and out of the ordinary. It supplies clients with an experience that is radically different from their daily lives. In the context of this experience, change not only becomes possible, it becomes probable. When clients come to therapy, we want to provide an atmosphere of possibility and wonder. We want to manifest a connection that is wonderfully uncommon and leads toward transformation. When we employ these elements in our work, we find that it easier to generate, not just effective results, but also healing at a much deeper level.

CHAPTER 5

THE MAGIC OF FRAMES

In our quest to create a magical session, it would be wise to become aware of the tendency to view the issues that our clients bring to us as isolated actions which have no context. It is not uncommon for therapists to first learn about a client's symptoms and, without proper understanding of the context in which the problem originates, then instantly move to a technical application to eradicate the symptoms. If we do not pay attention to the context, or the frame of reference where the problem originates, we may find that our techniques will not create the change we seek. I have come to believe that the frame of reference in which clients operate is often more important than the symptoms of the problem.

To comprehend the impact of frames of reference, we must first identify how we create these frames. All frames begin with the making of a distinction (Keeney, 1983). When a distinction is made, it creates a 'this' and a 'that.' If I say that someone has a psychological disorder, then I have drawn a distinction between 'a psychological disorder' and 'not a psychological disorder.' In order to make this distinction, I have to indicate what differences exist between the perceptions of 'a psychological disorder' and 'not a psychological disorder.' Clients come to therapy with distinctions they have made about their problem. It is important that, rather than taking clients' conclusions about these distinctions at face value, we explore what specific distinctions our clients have made about their problems. It is these very distinctions which create the reality they bring to therapy.

As humans, we are all prone to bias and these biases can shape how we view our world. This worldview that we created is based upon the distinctions that we draw. We believe we have a set reality due to our own distinctions, but in actuality, these distinctions merely give us a description of what we are observing. Once we draw a distinction about what we observe, we will usually create additional distinctions so that we can describe what it is we are observing (Bateson, 1979; Keeney, 1983). The distinctions are then linguistically labeled and become entities which we believe are 'real.' We are often unaware that our description of what we observe is not really what is being observed. We forget that there are many different distinctions which can be drawn about any situation we observe. Even though we draw these distinctions from reality, they are not reality in themselves.

From the drawing of our distinctions, we develop our own views about the world, and these views lead to our patterns of thought, emotion, and behavior. These patterns are confirmed and reinforced when we observe situations and interpret them as consistent with our worldview. These distinctions will also create a dichotomy in the mind of the observer so that observers will only see the distinctions of 'either/or' and will then only select one side as being correct. For them, there is no relationship between the two sides. The conclusion brought to therapy is dependent on the clients' own distinctions and observations. What may appear to be 'real' is usually much different from reality. These distinctions create personal frames of reference which then dictates the quality of their life.

In this light, it is easy to see that our values, our attitudes, our culture, and even our view of ourselves have been created by distinctions and conclusions which developed a frame of reference about the world. Our thoughts and feelings about areas such as connection, communication, love, and morality have been shaped by distinctions we have made based on our experiences. If we think of a frame of reference as a set of rules which govern one's perception of life and how one acts on that perception, it behooves therapists to recognize that everyone has a different frame of reference which supplies them with a way of understanding their world. Even though we may intellectually understand this assertion, our frames of reference stay intact due to the self-reflexive nature of the frames. These frames operate in a circular manner, in that they determine our perceptions of reality and simultaneously our perceptions will design our frames (Chenail et al., 2015).

Frames of reference are the context in which action takes place. Context determines how a person perceives and reacts to an event. The client's context includes, 'objective facts, the subjective appraisals of those facts and emotions driven by the client's schema dynamics (view of self, view of others, etc.). It is from a given context that ambivalence is created, problematic behaviors emerge, and solutions are discovered' (Mozdzrerz, Peluso, & Lisieck, 2014, p. 57). An event will be perceived differently by two different people based upon the context in which each places the action. For example, a heated argument between a husband and wife may be viewed as either a natural activity that occurs within relationships, the attempted domination of the wife by the husband, or the wife's attempt to emasculate the husband. The conclusion depends on the context in which the argument is placed. As Bateson (1979) stated, 'Without context, words and actions have no meaning at all. This is true not only of human communication in words, but also of all communication whatsoever, of all mental process, of all mind, including that which tells the sea anemone how to grow and the amoeba what he should do next' (p. 13).

Humans tend to believe that the frames which hold our worldview are the true reality. This can cause problems when we have become stuck in a frame that is filled with limitations and distress. We have the ability to create multiple and different frames, all of which showcase the perception to which we have ascribed. Once a frame has been established, all of the actions that occur within the frame will continue to maintain the frame. The problem that clients want to change cannot be changed if they remain within the same frame of reference. The problem is defined by the frame and therefore the problem is stuck in it. Essentially, the problem cannot be changed using the same inferences and interactions that created it.

Clients make a distinction between what is a problem and what is not a problem when they present therapists with their problem. Clients essentially have created a frame that identified a certain category of events as a problem. For example, when a client says that he is depressed and that everything he does is meaningless, he has created a frame of reference where any action he takes is filed into the category of 'meaningless.' He may try to do a multitude of solutions to his problem of depression, but none of these attempted solutions will have a major effect as long as he considers the actions that he takes as meaningless.

If we can adjust our clients' distinctions and their focus, then we can move away from their framing of their distinction as a problem.

If one views solving problems from the presupposition that: if 'A' is a problem for them, then 'not-A' will be the solution, then it may be difficult to create change. This is due to one being confined to a specific frame of dysfunction (the presence of A), and a distinction cannot exist without its complementary (Varela, 1979). As a result of this view of problem resolution, there will be attempts to do either more or less of A in a quest to solve A. If solutions are seen as the opposite of the problem in the 'A/not A' view of problem resolution, then change becomes more difficult since a problem has to have a solution which has to have a problem. Essentially, 'A' and 'not A' feed each other, and clients become stuck in a frame of reference in which the only way they know how to solve the problem is to do more of the same, thereby solidifying the problem. Our desire to rid ourselves of our problems sometimes chains us to the very thing we wish to abolish. Flemons (1991) reminds us that, 'Symptoms are haunting reminders that attempts to eradicate pieces of our lived experience, to banish parts of our minds, can unwittingly create and entrench the very problems we most dread. The parted mind does not, indeed cannot, depart' (p. 19).

Clients' frames will be difficult to change while they remain inside the frame. Clients who are stuck in their frames perceive all comments or actions by the therapist from the perspective of the frame. Therapists often have the experience of proposing new positive information to clients who either dismiss or ignore the validity of any comments made by the therapist. For example, a therapist may say to a depressed client, 'In spite of this situation you are going through, you are still a capable person who has much to offer the world.' The depressed client, firmly stuck inside the problem frame, replies back, 'I know, but I still can't shake the feeling that I have nothing of value to offer anyone.' The therapist's well-meaning attempt to adjust the negative cognition failed. Why? Because the comments were received within the same frame where the client is stuck. The more the therapist tries to change the problem from within the frame, the more difficult therapy becomes until finally the therapist gives up and tries something radically different, or labels the client, unfortunately, as 'resistant.'

Again, if the focus of therapy is based on the distinctions that clients make, then it is easy for both the therapist and the clients to become locked in the problem frame. What follows will be a continuous reinforcement of the clients' initial distinctions which keep change at bay (Chenail et al., 2015). However, suggestions of an alternative distinction by the therapist can lead to the creation of alternative frames of reference for clients. The more the original distinction is made the focal point of therapy, the more clients will perceive that the distinction is real and the problem will become more solidified in their consciousness. If client and therapist continue to focus on the distinction of a problem, this will contribute to maintaining the negative emotional state associated with the initial distinction (Kershaw & Wade, 2011).

The frame that has been set by clients holds all of their initial distinctions (Keeney, 1983). When a frame of despair becomes the dominant frame of how they perceive their world, this results in less than resourceful mental, emotional, and behavioral responses to the frame. Therapists have to be careful that they do not forget that any conversation within these frames, no matter from what theoretical orientation used, may contribute to the actual strengthening of the frame. Indeed, these frames may become more verified and solidified to clients due to extensive discussions of their problem as they continue to construct that which they are discussing. This is the danger using descriptions of pathology and diagnostic labeling since this can cement in our minds, and that of our clients, the idea that the problem *is* a problem. Therapists, instead, must offer alternative distinctions rather than also becoming locked into the clients' perceptions.

For example, a woman tells her therapist that she is a bad mother. The therapist asks what specifically makes her a bad mother. The woman says that she is a bad mother because she is divorced, she becomes too emotional when her children misbehave, and she spends little time with them due to her work responsibilities. At this point in the session, the woman has given the therapist a set of distinctions about what is a 'good mother' and what is a 'bad mother.' We can look at it like this:

Good Mother
She controls her emotions at all times
She has children who never misbehave
She always has time for her children
She is married

Bad Mother
She becomes upset when children misbehave
She has children who misbehave

She has to work many hours

She is divorced

The woman has created her own distinction which locks her into a reality in which she believes she belongs to the category of 'bad mother.' The woman has marked a boundary between good mother/bad mother. The problem with this marking is that any boundary drawn still connects both categories it is supposed to separate. A distinction cannot exist without its opposite value so there cannot be a category of good mother without having a category of bad mother. Trying to convince her to accept herself as a good mother instead of a bad mother creates a dichotomous struggle which can lock client and therapist into a frame of 'either/or' limitation. It would be more effective to offer information to the woman that will blur the boundary which causes her such emotional pain. Part of the discussion could go like this:

Woman: I yell and scream when the kids won't behave.

Therapist: Those kids must mean so much to you for you to get that passionate about them doing the right thing.

Woman: Yes, but I need to learn to not be so loud and angry.

Therapist: Sure, but it does let them know that you care enough about them that you will not be negligent and let them get into trouble. In fact, you are willing to really speak up to love and guide your kids.

The therapist is blurring the distinction because a 'bad mother' would not care enough about her children to speak up or to guide her children. The category she initially set did not account for the fact that a good mother can be both loud and caring. It will be more difficult for the woman to hold on to the distinction of 'good mother versus bad mother' if it is not as rigid as she originally envisioned. This rigidity which originally set the frame probably allowed for less than effective solutions for her conclusion that she is a bad mother. Her attempts to eradicate the either/or dichotomy only had cemented her place within the frame of 'bad mother.'

It is natural for anyone who is dealing with a problem to use a process to solve the problem, a process that may have worked previously. However, that process is often based on the frame of reference which we apply to the problem and this frame determines what we believe is an acceptable solution to be applied to the situation. Even if our attempts to apply the solution are not successful, we frequently will continue to apply the same solution, which, unfortunately, can worsen the very problem from which we are seeking relief. At this point, we may feel stuck and helpless as the solutions we apply continue to fail, which prompts us to do more of the same with similar results. With the same frame in place, any attempted solution will meet the same fate.

A problem occurs when both the client and the therapist are stuck in the same frame of reference. If the therapist's attempted solutions remain within the same frame which was brought to therapy, then therapy can be a frustrating and limiting experience. Therapists who also become locked into the frame will label both the problem and the attempted solutions as pathology, which will then maintain the frame that holds all the distinctions of that set. With the best of intentions, therapists may indirectly contribute to the continuation of the very problem from which clients want relief. As Chenail et al. (2015) state, 'Sometimes therapists are taught to keep clients inside pathological or problem themed contexts because their model needs that framing to be able to conduct its operations. Stated differently, a problem-focused therapist needs a problem in order to perform problem-solving' (p. 40).

Constantly focusing on a frame of pathology limits clients' access to empowering resources, which reside outside their frame. Unfortunately, most psychotherapy applications work primarily within the frame of pathology. Therapists are often taught to diagnose the problem and to work within the frame of the problem. The framing of problems as 'problems' leads therapists into a limited territory where anything inside the frame can become a potential problem. When psychotherapy is applied in this manner, therapists also lose access to resources that could help their clients. Viewing this from a functional perspective, 'all a practitioner needs to know is that any attention given to any part of the pattern or context that holds the problem will pragmatically contribute to keeping the problem in play' (Keeney & Keeney, 2013a, p. 25).

Since the very early days of psychotherapy, practitioners have been taught to seek out the root causes of pathology. Psychotherapy was designed to describe, understand, and diagnose human problems. When therapists work from a frame of pathology, less and less emphasis will be placed on the idea that healing can be brought about by anything other

THE MAGIC OF FRAMES

than mechanical applications or materialistic, biomedical solutions. We often overlook the cultural construction of diagnosing 'mental illness' and the importance of relational and interactional factors. If we frame all psychotherapy within a pathology frame, life's inevitable challenges such as relationships issues, disruptions in work, or existential angst are no longer normal passages in life, but rather they are things to be eradicated and possibly medicated. The very act of diagnosing creates a distinction which then in turn creates a frame of reference of pathology.

Due to the frame of pathology in which most therapists work, more practices are being shaped by an increasing standardization of applications, as well as a medicalized diagnostic system, and specific treatments which are erroneously labeled as 'evidence-based.' The appearance of natural symptoms to stressors such as grief, anxiety, and so on, are regarded as diseases that need to be eliminated, rather than natural aspects of the human condition. As Bradshaw (2012) stated when warning about new diagnosing proposals to the Diagnostic and Statistical Manual of Mental Disorders (DSM), 'Many complain that the proposals (to the DSM) so pathologize normal human actions that an unruly child's temper tantrum could be labeled "disruptive mood dysregulation disorder" or a mother's attempt to turn a child against the father in a custody dispute could be found to be suffering "parental alienation disorder"' (p. 3).

Unfortunately, therapists' need for reimbursement and desire for government funding for their work has increased medicalization and pathologizing of the psychotherapy field. As Elkins (2009) states, 'we have become so accustomed to describing psychotherapy in medical model terms that it's difficult, if not impossible, to remove the 'medical model grid' to see the process of psychotherapy as it actually is' (p. 268). If psychotherapy is a field that is based upon relational connection, then rigid interventions that are philosophically pathology centered are not suitable.

The advancing medicalization and standardization in the field prompted the British Psychological Society to proclaim (Bradshaw, 2012):

> The Society is concerned that clients and the general public are negatively affected by the continued and continuous medicalization of their natural and normal responses to their experiences; responses which undoubtedly

have distressing consequences which demand helping responses, but which do not reflect illnesses so much as normal individual variation. We believe that classifying these problems as 'illnesses' misses the relational context of problems and the undeniable social causation of many such problems.

(p. 3)

When the distinction of a 'problem' has been made for clients, they are frozen inside the frame of the problem and cannot move out of that frame. If they have fully committed to the belief that they have a problem, and their therapist shares this belief, the frame of pathology becomes locked and self-fulfilling. I have frequently observed that clients who have more trouble making changes in their lives are generally those who have so identified with their problem that they have taken on the identity of the problem. Their view of themselves is their diagnosis. It can be difficult to change the frame if clients are heavily invested in the identity of the frame. Even though they may want to change the actions that take place inside the frame, if their identity is the same as that of the problem, unconsciously, they may have become so invested in the maintenance of the frame that any attempt to change the frame may be met with every appearance of resistance.

Researchers have found that focusing sessions primarily on client problems do not result in more effectiveness in outcomes. It was found that when the focus was shifted to client resources, therapy could then progress toward its potential and improved significantly (Flückiger & Holtforth, 2008; Gassmann & Grawe. 2006). Viewing clients as having the ability to be able to change rather than focusing on client deficits aids in moving clients toward positive and healthy outcomes. In turn, a relentless focus upon client pathology can lead to less than positive outcomes for clients. As Gassmann and Grawe (2006) state, 'Unsuccessful therapists focused more on the patient's problems and tended to overlook the patient's resources. As could be seen from the patient's perspective, their self-confidence and positive rapport sank the longer the session lasted' (p. 9).

Decreasing the focus on the pathological frame of reference while opening up opportunities to explore areas of clients' lives will give therapists access to clients' strengths and resources which can activate the clients' inner healer. Therapists who decline in joining the problem and move clients outside of this frame, will find that opportunities appear which show that the original designation of the problem is not truly set in stone. The shifting of contexts to a more resourceful frame will create the conditions for a magical session to manifest. For this to happen, it is important to understand the order of change in which we are working.

ORDERS OF CHANGE

For our goal of a magical session, it would be wise to understand the level of change that we seek and how this relates to the clients' frame of reference. Orders of change in psychotherapy were first discussed by Watzlawick, Weakland, and Fisch (1974) and heavily influenced the field of family therapy. These researchers found that there are two orders of change: first-order and second-order. First-order change occurs within a specific frame of reference. This type of change occurs when therapists work inside the frame of the problem. First-order change is related to problem solving and to eradicating the clients' symptoms, and indeed, most psychotherapy models operate as first-order change models.

The following is an example of working from a first-order change perspective. A single mother brings her ten-year-old son to therapy due to the son's aggressive behavior and rudeness. The mother was divorced a year ago and has recently started dating. Her former marriage had been one in which she experienced some emotional and physical abuse, which her son had witnessed. The mother wants her son to stop being rude and aggressive toward her new boyfriend. She says that her boyfriend is a very kind man and does not deserve to be treated badly by her son. She wonders if therapy can help her son stop talking back and picking fights with her and her new boyfriend. The mother already has made a distinction about her son's behavior, and this distinction has created a frame of reference which labels the son as unruly and a 'bad boy.'

Approaching this case from a first-order change perspective would entail attempts to change the behavior, thoughts, and emotions within the frame of 'bad boy.' The therapist would instruct the mother to have better boundaries for her son. There would be a suggestion of using positive reinforcement in dealing with his behavior. Other therapy applications could include altering the mother's beliefs about her son's behavior or talking with her son about the thoughts which lead to his actions. All of these approaches are acceptable therapy applications, however, they all remain within the frame of a problem ('the bad boy').

To create transformational change, the frame of reference and the inferences that define it will have to change. When the frame has been adjusted, the actions which previously supported the old frame, now appear ineffective. When the problem occurs within a new frame, different actions are required and the patterns which solidified the problem become interrupted. This occurrence is known as second-order change.

Second-order change is change when there is an alteration in the specific frame of reference. Second-order change is a fundamental shift in the frame or the structure in which the problem occurs. It not only reduces symptoms, it transforms the system within which the symptoms operate. From a second-order perspective in the case of the 'bad boy,' the therapist comments to the mother how helpful it is that her son is testing the new boyfriend to determine if the boyfriend can deal with disagreement without resorting to violence. The therapist may also compliment the boy for protecting his mother from any potential harm, the type that he had witnessed in her marriage. The therapist may also muse aloud how devoted her son is to take such an interest in determining whether the new boyfriend is someone who will help her or hurt her. These assertions create new assumptions that lead to a different frame. The 'bad boy' is now seen as 'Mother's protector.' His rude or aggressive actions are now seen as resources in place to serve the family rather than to divide it.

Second-order change can be accomplished by changing the inferences which created the problem in the attempts to solve the problem. When the context of the problem is changed, it is conceivable that the actions or emotions that occur within the new frame could shift the assumptions which created the problem. Working toward second-order change requires that therapists recognize the complexity of human problems instead of a simple cause and effect reductionist view of change. Second-order change represents a radical shift in the system to a new and different level of functioning which may appear both sudden and illogical.

It is necessary that the therapist move beyond standardized interventions due to the first-order limitations which they entail. Being stuck within a scripted way of responding to a specific problem can limit therapists in examining the unique frames of reference of the clients. Therapists may be distracted and miss possible resources which clients possess. When therapy is limited to a scattering of techniques which have been marketed as 'evidence-based,' therapists run the risk of over-looking the uniqueness of each individual client and this may lead to ineffective outcomes. If there is no consideration of the distinctions, the conclusions, and the frames in which clients operate, therapy becomes a soulless endeavor in which rote therapy maneuvers become the standard and clients who do not fit into the standard created by therapists are labeled as 'resistant' or 'chronic.'

Second-order change can also be created by altering the actions which occur within the frame of reference to an action that is radically different. Remember, if the actions within the frame do not match the assumptions that create the frame, then the frame can change. For example, rather than telling a married couple to avoid the relentless arguments which brought them to therapy, the therapist could direct the couple to have their arguments only at a specific location. Further, they must pantomime their grievances. Because the frame of what is appropriate has been set in the clients' minds, the adjustment of the actions within the frame redefines the rules of the frame. The inference from which the problem was created is changed and the frame becomes dismantled.

From the second-order perspective, directives to clients may often appear nonsensical since this is an attempt to solve problems from a different frame of reference. Asking clients to take an action outside their present frame may seem odd to them, because, 'The alternatives that arise in second-order change represent a whole new set. Because they do not reflect the person's current worldview, they are commonly experienced by the individual or participants trapped in a vicious or first-order cycle as strange, weird, out of the blue, paradoxical – often contrary to common sense' (Fraser & Solovey, 2007, p. 26).

I once worked with a young woman I will call Britney. She had developed a compulsive pattern of knocking on a wall seven times any time she thought about or heard about any health-related topic. These topics caused her to create frightening scenarios of becoming sick, having to be rushed to the hospital, and then eventually dying. These frightening thoughts and images caused her to have intense feelings of panic, which oddly enough, were only alleviated (albeit momentarily) by knocking on a wall seven times. This pattern of behavior had begun to consume her throughout the day and she felt trapped by this compulsive behavior. She interacted with people less frequently due to her odd behavior which also caused her great embarrassment. Britney felt that she was on a daily rollercoaster trying to avoid any situation which would trigger her feelings of panic. She also had to step out of her office area at work in order to privately complete her ritual of knocking.

After listening to her story and collecting the preliminary information about her situation, I told Britney that I was not going to ask her to stop knocking on walls when she felt panic. I explained to her that my asking her to stop an activity so intense would probably not work. Britney agreed with my assessment. I explained to her that I merely wanted her to commit to doing one jumping jack between each of her seven knocks. At first, she thought that I was joking, but eventually she agreed to follow my request for one week. I also asked her to keep a log of each time that she had the overwhelming desire to knock on the wall seven times so that we could chart her progress throughout the week.

When Britney returned for her next session two weeks later, she informed me that she had been able to stop knocking so often. She had followed my directive for a week and soon discovered that the required jumping jacks had slowed her pattern of behavior down. Also, the whole situation seemed more absurd that she had previously been able to acknowledge. Her log of knocking showed a steady decrease in the number of times she needed to knock on walls. She also said that the number of intrusive thoughts about health-related issues had declined. She admitted that she still had some thoughts about illness which bothered her, but they were not nearly as intense or as disabling as they had been. Her frame of reference had evolved from 'illness panic ritual' to 'absurd and annoying ritual.' My request that she do jumping jacks had not made sense in her previous frame.

Another example of a second-order changing of action dismantling a frame took place with a client I will call Hank, who came to therapy because of his pornography addiction. Hank had become more and more addicted to watching pornography over the last few years, and it had begun to take a toll on his marriage. His wife had found out and was very distressed since it appeared that he desired pornography more than he desired her. Hank believed that he could not contain himself because he instantly sought pornography anytime that he was left alone. He felt that he was out of control and his wife had taken on the role of parent monitoring him constantly except when she had to work. Her actions seemed to make his addiction worse and resentment toward each other was growing deeper.

Much as I had done with Britney, I told Hank that I could not ask him to stop this activity, so I was not going to try to do so. However, I asked him if he could help me to understand the triggers that pushed him to seek pornography. He agreed to do anything that was asked of him because he was terrified of losing his wife. Hank was very motivated to change since his wife threatened to leave him due to his addiction. He desperately wanted to quit, but he felt helpless and unable to change his behavior.

I asked him to keep a detailed log of everything that took place during the previous half hour as soon as he thought about pornography. He was to complete this log before he began watching pornography. In a spreadsheet, Hank was to write down the day of the week, the time of day, the temperature, the room he was sitting in, the clothes he was wearing, the thoughts he had been thinking over the past ten minutes, the bodily sensations he was aware of, how many times he had had something to drink, what he had eaten at his last meal, what time he woke up that morning, where he had been earlier, the last person he had spoken to on the phone and what was discussed, and how many times he had gone to the bathroom. Hank was allowed to watch pornography only after he completed writing down all of the requested information. This whole process would take a couple of minutes. Hank agreed to log all this information and was told to return with his information within two weeks.

In two weeks, Hank came back to his session, he had dutifully logged all the information as he had been requested. In going over his information, I noticed that Hank had decreased his logging of information after the first week. When I asked about this, Hank said that he had felt less motivated to watch pornography because of the time it took for him to complete his log. I pretended to be concerned about how little he was logging information and watching pornography. I told Hank that I wanted to be sure that this was not a fluke, so he should continue gathering the information about triggers. I then told him to continue his assignment for another week. When Hank came in a week later, he confessed that he had only watched pornography one time, and that it did not feel the same to him. After another round of two weeks of the logging of information, he found that he rarely watched pornography anymore and had found other things to do instead of the tedious process of logging information. The frame of 'pornography addict' was deconstructed due to the disruption of the patterns which held the frame together.

A magical session is one in which the clients' frames of anguish are dismantled and transformed into new empowering frames for living. Since our frames of reference determine our quality of life, even pain can be a resource within a different frame. Being healed does not always mean not having symptoms. Our depression can be a catalyst for greater insights into our nature of being. Our anxieties can be wake-up calls to inform us of where we have been ignoring some crucial aspects of living authentically. Healing occurs when we are freed from disabling frames of reference. We no longer view symptoms as immobilizing.

When the inevitable turmoil that life can bring is framed as insurmountable or as punishment, the results can be psychological immobilization in one's personal development. However, if the same turmoil is framed as being part of the 'Hero's Journey' which every individual undertakes, then the same situation can have radically different outcomes. There is a tremendous difference when the causes of the symptoms of depression are being labeled as a dysfunctional attachment narrative instead of being part of the creative journey an artist takes through life. A shift in perception or of meaning by clients, allows for a change in the context of the situation. Problems are understood and experienced differently when the context has been adjusted. If clients no longer see the problem as the 'problem,' then it does not matter if troubling actions continue since their meaning is no longer the same. As Keeney (1983) states, 'A lens, or frame of reference determines the pattern we see, whether it is up or down, distorted or not. A change of lens always invokes a period of initial confusion or transition. If an observer can endure the crisis of transition, a new frame will result in an alternative order' (p. 155).

I once had a client I will call Gene who was dealing with social anxiety issues and panic attacks due to a variety of factors. Gene had graduated from high school and had started college, but he began to have emotional issues which required him to leave school. He returned to his parents' home and continued to live there for the past couple of years. He helped his mother around the house and took care of his father who was in poor health. He had noticed that his anxiety had become worse over the past couple of years and this anxiety caused him to avoid going out and interacting with others.

Gene told me that he was very worried about running into people that he used to know before he started having anxiety. He felt they would observe how little he had advanced in his life. He said he knew he was depressed. He also believed that it was not good to talk to former friends because he 'did not want to burden them' with his problems. Gene did not want to make anyone feel bad due to his issue. When he did go out, he sometimes had panic attacks which caused him to immediately return home. This cycle of attempting to go out, having a panic attack, and then going home feeling defeated, caused Gene to feel stuck and more depressed.

As Gene described his situation, it became clear that his frame of reference was one of guilt and shame. He would go out, have an anxiety attack, and then feel a sense of shame about how his anxiety issue kept him from progressing as his peers. He would then have anxiety about the potential of seeing one of his peers when he went out, which caused additional panic for him. This pattern kept him stuck at his parents' home. His only positive emotion was that he was glad he could help his parents while he was staying with them.

When I heard Gene say that he didn't want to 'burden others' with his problems, I thought about how a desire to not burden someone else was actually an act of compassion. I told him that his concern for how other people feel was quite remarkable. I complimented him on how compassionate he was to willingly allow himself to suffer in silence so that others would not suffer. I told him it was possible that his unconscious mind could even be creating these panic episodes to help shield others from feeling his pain. He responded favorably to my conjectures. Our conversation on compassion continued as we discussed many other examples of the times that he was kind to others. We discussed the spiritual role of compassion and the many historical figures who had shown great compassion while going through their own hardships. The topic of compassion was a different frame in which to see his 'problem.'

I explained to Gene that it was not fair to waste his compassion being alone at home. We had to devise some way for him to help others with his strong sense of compassion. I told him that he had much to teach all of us about how to become more compassionate in our lives. I reminded him about the hardships of the various compassionate historical figures as they spread their messages of hope to others. I let him know that he could not fully show compassion by staying at home.

He needed to find somewhere to interact with others on a small scale to help them learn to have compassion.

Gene agreed that this was important work to do. Within one month, Gene had begun to volunteer to deliver food to senior citizens who had little money and were unable to leave their homes. He also started running small errands to help his parents. Gene decided to contact one of his friends from high school and they went to a movie together. In time, he found that when he did go out he was not as nervous as before and he discovered that he could interact with people with fewer panic episodes. The changing of the frame of reference from anxiety/guilt/shame to the frame of compassion caused his reality to readjust. His previously self-defeating fear was now a source of compassion to be shared with others

I have found that therapy sessions can become magical if therapists are not mired down in a pathology related framing of problems. Spending too much time on superfluous details in an ongoing search for etiology can rob sessions of their magic. Moving clients out of the frames in which they feel stuck, allows clients to access the resources which will enable them to solve their own problems. The more we focus on conversation drenched in pathology, the more we remain in a pathology laden frame. After we have fully listened to and honored the stories our clients bring to therapy, we need to change the direction away from where clients' attention is being absorbed.

Second-order change requires that we assist clients to maneuver out of their stories. The frame will not be changed by excessive discussion within a frame of disempowerment. The self-reflexive nature of frames will only continue building onto itself. It is only when we leave the frame altogether that we can more easily connect with the wealth of inner resources that our clients possess. Moving out of problem frames and activating clients' inner resources not only emphasizes their potential for changing, but it also can have a calming effect on clients as they feel their strengths and capabilities are being recognized by the therapist, rather than a view of clients based in pathology (Caspar & Berger, 2012).

DEFICIT THEMES VS. TRANSFORMATIONAL THEMES

If we were to view the frames of reference that clients bring to therapy as movie themes, it would be easier to adjust clients' limiting frames.

For example, you may have seen the following 'movies' in your therapy room:

'The Man Who Cannot Forgive'
'The Woman Who Is Scared'
'The Child Who Terrorizes the Family'
'The Past that Haunts'
'The Controlling Parent'
'The Spouse Who Cheats'

As long as therapy is stuck in clients' themes, anything that operates *within* that theme will be *part* of the theme (Chenail et. al, 2015). It is not enough to understand how the movie got started, who the players are, what scenes have taken place, or what will be the future scenes, we have to change the theme of the movie. This necessitates a move *out of the frame of pathology* and *into a frame of possibility*. We must move away from themes that are focused on client deficits and move into new themes which focus on client transformation. Since the theme (frame) is what makes the movie, then the way to transformation is to make a totally different movie instead of changing the lines and the characters in the present one.

An example of changing from a deficit theme to a transformational theme would be my work with a client I will call Jamie. Jamie was a 28-year-old male who came to therapy because of his impending divorce. He loved his wife, however, she was not interested in continuing the marriage. He admitted that a part of him did not want to continue the marriage either, yet the situation was still very difficult for him. Jamie reported having feelings of intense sadness, grief, and loss. He told me that he was uncertain about any aspect of his future. Jamie was not sleeping well and he had not been able to focus much on his work. He admitted that he had been slowly isolating himself from his friends and family.

If I had to select a theme to Jamie's movie, it would be 'The Abandoned Man with No Future.' This may have been a profound movie for those viewers with existentialist leanings, but it was not a movie in which Jamie enjoyed being the principal actor. Any action that occurred inside the movie was still tied to its themes of abandonment, isolation, and uncertainty. Any directive that I gave within this theme would be tied to the very theme Jamie wanted to end.

As we were talking, I could not help but notice that Jamie had a very quick and sharp wit. He made jokes about feeling uncomfortable and being alone, and he told that me he always had been good at dark humor. I asked him if he ever shared any of his humor with others. Jamie smiled and told me that he once wanted to be a stand-up comic and a voice actor. I was surprised to hear this and our discussion moved into a conversation about what he liked about comedy. We discussed how he might consider doing some comedy sketches about the uncomfortable issues with which he was wrestling. Jamie was open to this idea and made plans to post some videos on social media of himself doing a one- or two-minute comedy routine. We spent the remainder of our session brainstorming how he could get more people to watch his videos.

When Jamie returned for his next session, he appeared to be more emotionally stable. He smiled more and said that he had been able to sleep more. He was excited that the response to his videos had been mostly positive and he found that he had been interacting well with some friends lately. He spent the rest of the session telling me what short-term and long-term goals he had for his comedy work. He wanted to eventually leave his present job and work more in the entertainment industry. Jamie was still sad about his divorce, but he was feeling more empowered. The movie theme of his life changed from 'The Abandoned Man with No Future' to now being 'The Adventures of a New Comedian.' Any new actions he took within this new frame could be used to empower him and his career.

Working from this perspective may seem contrary to the training most of us received in graduate school. Most psychotherapists are taught to stay within the problem drenched themes which clients bring to their sessions. Unfortunately, much of our training hampers us our being able to spot the natural strengths and the resources which clients possess, and when they are spotted, many of us fail to utilize them effectively in our work. As Keeney and Keeney (2013a) state, 'Perhaps the biggest secret in therapy is that a strict focus on resources, accompanied by no unnecessary attention given to problems or solutions, is the most transformative way to handle a client's stuck life situation' (p. 42). Working outside the frame of a problem allows us to help our clients create new themes. These themes then become self-reflexive and empower clients to obtain the resources which can help them transcend their present problem.

Another client, Alan, came to therapy after the death of his wife. His wife had been ill for a long time and Alan had taken time away from his construction business to take care of her. However, Alan's wife had to have many expensive procedures, several of which their insurance did not cover, and this had created a financial hardship situation. Alan's inability to be present at his business eventually cost him several important contracts. He was devoted to his wife, but unfortunately, he paid a financial price for his devotion because his business had to declare bankruptcy. He had to sell his own home and had to move his ailing wife into his parents' home in order to provide her with medical care.

After his wife died, Alan went into a deep depression. He had not only lost his life partner, but he literally had no money. His business was defunct, and he was barely able to get out of bed in the morning. A very independent man, having to live with his parents at this stage of his life troubled him greatly. He was lost and felt like a failure. He admitted to me that sometimes he felt he had nothing to live for and he wanted to 'check out' of life. Coming to therapy was something that he had resisted previously, but now he realized that if he didn't get help, then he might not make it much longer.

Listening to Alan's story of losing his livelihood, his home, and his wife, I could not help but see his present theme as 'The Man Who Lost It All.' This theme was not only disempowering, it was hopeless. I doubted that we even would be able to get into the deep level of grief that Alan was experiencing. Working inside the theme of his loss would not move Alan into a more resourceful state to effectively handle his grief. I realized that to help Alan we had to quickly move out of the movie theme of 'The Man Who Lost It All.'

I had noticed that he appeared to be much more animated when he discussed the operation of his now defunct business. Alan had taken pride in how well he treated his customers and wished that he could have been more successful. Brief signs of life appeared in his eyes when he talked about how he set up worksites and how he monitored the workers who built the buildings. He seemed to have enjoyed interacting with the customers and hated that he disappointed many of them when he could not accommodate them during his wife's final months.

After I sat with Alan and fully listened to his story, I told him that I aware of how much the loss of his wife had devastated him. I then paused and said, 'Alan, I can't imagine how much it must have hurt to lose her. Having said that, I think that right now the biggest issue you have is not her death.' Alan looked surprised at what I had said. I continued, 'I believe that the biggest challenge you have now is that you have to get back into business.' Alan perked up immediately.

'Alan, you are supposed to be helping people in this area who believe in you. That seems to be your mission in life. I wonder if one of the main reasons you feel so bad is that you are not in the business of helping others.' Alan thought for a minute and then agreed. He accepted the change of the theme from 'The Man Who Lost It All' to a new theme of 'Back in Business.' We began to work on solutions within a new frame of reference, which would inspire him and would give him emotional resources which would help as he worked through his grief. We decided that he would meet with lenders who had previously worked with him to see if they could help him start his new business. I suggested that he could use his wife's initials somewhere in the name of his new company. This idea touched him deeply, and between our sessions, he sat down and created a business plan with a new name for his company which honored the memory of his late wife. At our next session, Alan said that he had felt more energy and focus than he had in months. He also had some positive news from one of his lenders. In time, Alan would process his emotions about his wife's passing, but he would do it within a new positive theme of possibility and opportunity rather than loss and despair.

Few people ever achieve transformational change while they are still stuck in the themes of distress and excessive exploration of distressed themes only leads to more distress. After clients have told their stories and have felt supported and understood by the therapist, then work will need to commence on moving them out of those themes of disempowerment. I have seen rapid, magical changes in many clients when therapy is allowed to move to a second-order change. Our best techniques become supercharged when we are unchained from narrow, constricted, and unhelpful frames.

CHAPTER 6

THE MAGIC OF NONLINEAR THINKING

Therapists often take shortcuts in which they create simple explanations for events. This is natural as we all enjoy tidy, simple answers to questions that challenge us. The desire to break down an event to only one element, and then label that particular element as the cause of a problem is certainly alluring. Many in the psychotherapy marketplace have decided that they have determined what that one element is. Whether it is an element found in one's cognitions, one's behaviors, or one's emotions, these purveyors of the latest and greatest new theory or technique focus on the importance of this one element. They then go on to identify the one element they favor as the primary cause for client problems. This assertion is then used to create a new, specific method of therapy. Thus, a new therapeutic maneuver is born built on the premise that a single element is the root cause of humanity's emotional suffering.

In spite of how logical this may sound, clinicians' habitual citing of linear causes for client problems may mistakenly miss other elements which could benefit clients. Setting the necessary conditions for magical sessions requires a shift away from strictly linear thinking. In order to have the maximum flexibility and creativity in working with problems, it is important that therapists are open to nonlinear thinking when approaching problems. It is by abandoning the predictable ways of responding to client problems that we can open the door to a magical session.

Linear thinking is when we determine that there is a logical connection between the cause of one thing to the effect of another thing.

Using linear thinking, a therapist looks for the simplest channel that will create the desired solution. The solution to clients' problems is perceived as a short and direct path in which the therapist is already aware of the outcome of the intervention at the beginning of the therapy process. The therapist then believes achieving the outcome is simple if one follows a predetermined set of steps from where clients are presently to where clients want to be.

A linear view asserts that 'A' causes 'B.' This way of thinking sees all action by 'B' connected to 'A' as its cause. From the linear perspective, the endpoint in a sequence or the result is predetermined, and one follows a series of clear-cut steps to arrive at the end point. Always tracing backwards to 'A' means the sequence will always have the same predictable outcome through the calculable and standardized process. This sequential set of steps results in a predetermined, predictable course. If 'A' causes 'B,' then 'B' will cause 'C,' and so on.

Linear thinking uses reductionism as a base for problem-solving. Reductionism focuses on details within the problem and then takes the problem apart by studying the parts of the problem (and then studying the parts of the parts of the parts!). Reductionism attempts to find a solution by analyzing the smallest part. This linear perspective in modern Western thought has its roots in the Enlightenment of the seventeenth century from when the scientific method was born. This linear view proposed that any process was structured in a definite, fixed fashion. Events that are sequenced in a linear way work from the premise that one event can directly and independently cause another event. This perspective was taken up by most psychotherapies as the proponents sought to find a root cause for all of humankind's mental distresses. For example, in psychoanalysis, 'unconscious conflicts' cause problems, in cognitive therapy, 'cognitive distortions' cause problems, and in client-centered therapy, 'conditions of worth' cause problems.

At some level, viewing a psychotherapy case from a linear perspective may be effective, but it can also limit the clinician's ability to formulate generative interventions. It would be more useful for therapists to view their cases by moving beyond a simple equation of 'this' causes 'that.' A focus on a specific part of an event without any attention paid to the connections between the parts can lead to the specific part of the problem to be seen as an isolated 'cause.' This simple cause and effect perspective removes any questions concerning the nature of the relationship between the parts of the system. It can also reduce therapy to an oversimplified intervention solely rooted in linear and logical problem-solving. This will not work with every case that therapists encounter.

Nardone and Balbi (2008) relate a story of a psychiatrist in Germany who was treating a man in a psychiatric unit who constantly disturbed the patients and staff because of his incessant clapping. When approached by a psychiatrist and asked about why he was constantly clapping, the man told the psychiatrist that he had to clap in order to keep elephants away. The psychiatrist attempted to use linear logic to help the man understand that there were no elephants in the hospital nor in any part of Germany. The man smiled as he continued clapping and said there indeed was proof that his clapping was working. The psychiatrist's attempt to solve the problem by a linear means only resulted in solidifying the problem. The psychiatrist's linear problem-solving attempt was based on his view that 'A' (irrational thought) causes 'B' (clapping), did not take into consideration that the man's logic was not standard logic!

One of the limitations of a linear approach to therapy is that complex phenomena are sometimes reduced to overly simplistic explanations and applications which may limit results. Linear solutions reduce human behavior to a mechanical process while offering the hope of predictability for the psychotherapist. This reductionist process can sometimes give insights about the specific part of the problem being examined, but it does not help much with understanding the 'whole.' When reductionism is applied,

> [it] takes a multi-dimensional and complex phenomenon and confines it to one specific or (too) few dimensions. This could be the reduction of emergent phenomena (e.g., life, consciousness, or interpersonal structures) to reputed underlying subsidiary systems or components, which, taken to its extreme, results in materialism or physicalism. In other words, reductionism views the world from a point of view that does not consider the possibilities of other approaches or theories of reality.
>
> (Schiepek, Eckert, Aas, Wallot, & Wallot, 2015, p. 3)

A different perspective to take when working with clients is to approach cases from nonlinear thinking. If linear thinking focuses on how 'A' causes 'B,' nonlinear thinking is more concerned with exploring other different paths to an end. Nonlinear thinking enables therapists to observe situations from multiple viewpoints and to appreciate how different elements interact within a networked pattern to produce a result. Nonlinear thinking takes into consideration how the environment can affect an individual and how an individual can affect an environment. This perspective allows and encourages therapists to move away from 'A' causes 'B,' if warranted, and to investigate different possibilities and options.

Nonlinear thinking is less restrictive and less rigid than linear thinking because it welcomes creativity. If there is uncertainty about what factor causes what event, nonlinear thinking allows for the bigger picture of client problems. This can increase our ability to obtain a wider variety of outcomes. Linear interventions which only utilize logic will not always be effective, as the example of the man who clapped to keep elephants away shows us. With a lack of predetermined planning, nonlinear interventions allow room for maneuvering to unknown areas.

I once worked with a woman named Beth, who had a history of psychiatric disorders. She had seen several therapists and psychiatrists over the years due to her hallucinations and the fears caused by these hallucinations. She lived with her mother, her daughter, and her granddaughter. Beth had worked in the medical field for several years before she began to have mental health issues and she was on disability. Because of her knowledge and experience in the medical field, Beth refused to take any medication because of potential side effects. Beth had attempted therapy previously, but she stated the cognitive-based interventions that her therapists recommended did not help her. She had done her best to manage her emotional state; however, in the last few months she began to have a new and terrifying hallucination.

Beth had begun to see a creature in her bedroom. She described the creature as having a lizard-like body and a lion-shaped head. This creature frightened her and she was afraid to go into her bedroom. She eventually returned to her bedroom, but the creature would still appear in the corner and hiss at her. This sight greatly troubled Beth who, even though she knew it was a hallucination, she felt powerless to deal with this new situation. Her home had been turned upside down because of her latest vision and her granddaughter had become afraid as a result of Beth's fear. Beth's daughter was angry at her mother because Beth's behavior frightened the granddaughter. Beth's mother was upset with Beth's daughter because of her lack of understanding of Beth's condition. This new hallucination was indeed wreaking havoc in her life.

If we assumed a linear thinking case conceptualization, Beth's problem would be categorized as her hallucinations (A) causes her fear (B). Although correct, this 'A' to 'B' progression leaves us locked into only one solution for Beth's problem: we must change or get rid of 'A.' This would be difficult due to Beth's reluctance to take medication. Her lack of response to the traditional therapy approaches was also an obstacle. From this linear perspective, we are locked into a way of a situation with limited options. If, however, we allow ourselves to look beyond the linear, we can shift the emphasis from strictly getting rid of the problem. Our new emphasis shifts from eradicating an undesirable part of a person's existence to the relationship one has to that part.

Hearing that Beth's creature hissed at her and had a lion-shaped head, I asked Beth if the creature was more like a cat or lizard. She told me that it seemed more like a cat. I then asked if she knew that cats usually hiss when they are frightened. Beth thought for a moment and then said that she had heard this as well. I then asked her, was it is possible that this creature could be trapped in her bedroom and was afraid that she might harm it? This was a new and odd idea for Beth. I then said that perhaps she should approach the creature as if it were a hurt and frightened animal. I let her know that there is a possibility that the creature wants to leave but feels trapped. I also recommended that Beth bring the creature a bowl of milk as a sign of good faith that she was not going to hurt the creature. I told her it was probably a good idea to involve her granddaughter, as long as she told the granddaughter that they were just 'playing pretend.' Beth's granddaughter would not then be afraid. Beth thought about this request and said that she would try it to see what would happen.

Returning to therapy a couple of weeks later, Beth told me that she still saw the creature in her bedroom, but it is not hissing quite as much. She and her granddaughter play a new game of 'make-believe' and would put out a bowl of milk for the 'pretend creature' (which was still very real to Beth) daily. Beth reported that her granddaughter did not appear afraid any longer and her own daughter was being much nicer to Beth. Beth's mother had also stopped fussing over Beth's daughter. Overall, the home was much more peaceful. In time, Beth began to see the creature less and less. When she did see the creature, it merely looked at her without any fearful reactions, as Beth put in 'Just like an old, sleepy cat.' A nonlogical and nonlinear way approach to Beth's problem was necessary to create a change in how she related to her problem.

From a nonlinear perspective, humans do not inhabit vacuums. They are affected by their surroundings and then they affect their surroundings. At some level, there is a cause and effect process in the relationship that humans have to their environment, but it is rarely a linear one, nor is it consistently predictable. The interactions humans have with their environment is not a process that can be explained in strict 'if' and 'then' conclusions. A nonlinear perspective moves therapists away from a view of humans as a type of mechanism. Instead, therapists will see them as a network of integral patterns of relationships. In nonlinear thinking, we do not see clients in terms of simplistic actions, but rather we see patterns, relationships, and the contexts within which these patterns and relationships exist. Thinking in a nonlinear fashion, 'means that a person sees beyond the facts to the patterns that emerge and realizes that there may be more to a situation than is presented on the surface' (Mozdzierz, Peluso, & Lisiecki, 2014, p. 2).

Operating from a nonlinear perspective also helps therapists to understand that no one event independently causes another event. Events have what Bateson (1979) referred to as 'recursive causality.' This means that processes circle around to where they began and can simultaneously create both cause and effect. Action taken in the present will be fed into the future. This creates a circular interaction between the action occurring in the moment and the effect it will have on the environment, which will then be fed back to alter future action. The parts of the sequence have a mutual influence upon each other and serve to create more complex actions. This explanation helps us to see relationships between multiple parts rather than accepting simply event 'A' causes event 'B.'

Think about how our brains can be thought of as an anticipatory system which, due to our experiences, develops our assumptions, which in turn shapes how we emotionally react to our world. Our past experiences then circle back to direct our reactions to future experiences. As these emotional reactions to our assumptions persist, they become automatically ingrained. They will further function as 'attractor states' which serve to 'help the system organize itself and achieve stability.

Attractor states lend a degree of continuity to the infinitely possible options for activation profiles' (Siegel, 1999, p. 218). These attractors continue to influence us by drawing us toward specific patterns which our past experience has ingrained in our memory and continue to govern how we interact with our world in the future (Hill & Rossi, 2017).

For example, a husband yells at his wife, who then yells back at her husband. The husband may feel invalidated by the wife's yelling back and the wife may feel bullied by the husband's yelling. If we look at this example from a linear perspective, the husband by yelling (A) causes the wife to yell back (B). This linear approach may work to show a progression of actions, but it does not fully explain the entire situation. The interaction between the husband and the wife involves feedback from their former action involving cause (A) and effect (B) to recursively act on each other to create a more complex situation (invalidation and a sense of being bullied). The response of the wife to the husband may confirm for him that his emotions are being invalidated. The wife's response to the husband is due to her perception that by his yelling, she is being bullied which in turn sets in motion her reaction to him. The parts 'A' and 'B' working together create an outcome that is greater than the individual parts. The wife may come to expect yelling from her husband and will be ready to yell back at him. The husband expects his wife to yell at him which solidifies his emotional response to her. This process then moves to a higher level of complexity known as 'resentment,' which now is too complex to simply reverse. If the husband stopped yelling, there is no indication that the couple's resentment would suddenly disappear merely because the perceived initial cause of the husband's yelling ceased.

Bateson's concept of recursive causality is similar to the theory of autopoiesis. This theory, proposed by Maturana and Varela (1987), defined a living system as one which recursively reproduces itself. Different elements of a system interact in a certain way so that the system produces, and then reproduces, those different elements. This self-reproduction process is operationally closed, however, this does not mean that the system does not interact with the outside environment. It merely means that no operations can enter or leave the system from the outside of the system. An example of autopoiesis is the self-reproduction of cells. Cells reproduce elements of themselves as molecules, proteins, and so on. The production of these elements may come from within the cells, but in order to exist, cells need energy from the environment. The cells' system, however, decides through what medium the energy is exchanged with the environment.

Even though we are taught to view life from a cause and effect schematic, nature itself rarely operates in those terms. Let's examine the growth of an oak tree. A linear explanation for this is easy, but it is woefully incomplete. If we say that the oak tree comes from an acorn, this is only partially true. Yes, an oak tree can grow from an acorn, but without other elements in the process, the tree will not develop. The acorn alone does not create the tree. The acorn must have soil. The soil needs a certain amount of moisture and acidity to facilitate growth. The soil also needs adequate sunlight to produce an oak tree. Once the tree is fully grown, it continues to need all of those elements to continue as an oak tree. Essentially, the oak tree is a complex process which would cease if any one of these elements were taken away. A simple explanation of an acorn is not sufficient to fully comprehend an oak tree.

Since living systems are self-reproducing networks, they undergo continuous changes in their structure while at the same time maintaining their organizational patterns. Because these systems are self-organizing, they respond to their environment in a manner governed by their own levels of organization. Our cells give rise to our tissues, out of which comes our organs, out of which comes our bodies, out of which comes our person, out of which comes a family, out of which comes a community, out of which comes a country, out of which comes a continent, out of which comes a planet. This nonlinear systemic view of nature suggests that any attempt to separate human cognition, emotion, and behavior from the environment from which it arises is short-sighted. Even though the lure of the easy 'one size fits all' therapy is appealing, it often neglects the reality of a dynamic, living human organism. As therapists, we should ask ourselves are we truly able to fit all human behavior into a simple cause and effect, no-fail process? Too often, therapists locked into the dissection a specific part of a client's existence, lose sight of the importance of the whole. To borrow a popular phrase, they miss the forest due to their focus on the trees.

Therapy is in itself a holistic process. Unfortunately, many theories reduce clients to being parts, while ignoring the whole. These parts may be labeled as 'cognitive distortions,' 'overly reactive amygdala,' 'defense mechanisms,' or 'weak ego strength,' but humans are open, complex systems. The complexity of a system occurs when the system has a wide variety of parts, yet those parts are interdependent. The totality or whole which emerges from the combination of all these parts is naturally much more than any one single part.

Here is an example of how cause and effect appear easy to discern, however, this perception can be deceptive when we overlook the importance of 'parts.'

If the question is asked, what makes a bus go, the simple response may be the answer, 'gas.' This response may be correct on one level, but it also lacks a more complete view of the question. Granted, the bus won't go if there is no gas, but there are other factors that may prevent the bus from going, even if gas is present. A few other answers could be:

- The bus will not go if the ignition is not activated.
- The bus will not go if there are changes in its schedule.
- The bus will not go if there is not a driver present.
- The bus will not go if there are no tires on the vehicle.
- The bus will not go if no one wants to ride the bus.

All of these answers could contribute to a 'cause' for the 'effect' of the bus not going.

As therapists, I believe that it is important to be mindful of the great complexity in our clients and our therapeutic interventions will need to reflect this complexity. We are all individuals, yet we also constantly interact with other individuals. We are all parts of a larger 'whole' that has increasing levels of complexity. Our parts of the 'whole' communicate, which allows us to be both self-correcting and self-organizing. Our 'whole' takes in information from both internal and external sources, which is organized into a hierarchy of organizational levels. This organization of different levels makes simple cause and effect and linear-based therapy rather limited. Humans are far too complex to be understood in simple cause and effect terms. Since humans constantly interact with their environments, they have the ability to constantly create new 'wholes.' The emerging 'wholes' cannot be understood from observing only the isolated parts.

From a nonlinear perspective, it becomes difficult to rigidly structure therapy interventions in a 'do X when Y happens' process. Instead of studying the parts of the parts of the parts of a problem, it behooves us to be more resourceful in our interventions while considering the greater whole. Rather than focusing on one part as the 'cause,' we should take a larger view of the interaction which will provide us with more opportunities to create change. We are trapped by problems if we apply linear thinking as we attempt to solve the problems. Our continuing to try and solve the problem in the same predictable linear ways only makes the problem worse. When we approach problems from a nonlinear perspective, we are able to access potential resources beyond the boundary of what is immediately apparent.

Let us examine one of my cases through the lens of both linear thinking and nonlinear thinking.

Adam, a 14-year-old boy, was brought to therapy by his parents because of his truancy from school, his reports of depression, and his emotional outbursts. His mother, who was a psychologist, believed that Adam had a mild form of autism. Her diagnosis of her son led to both the mother and her husband feeling sorry for Adam and catering to his every whim. They reported that overall Adam had been a very good child up until the last year.

Adam was polite and appeared to be a very intelligent boy. He said that when he thought about going to school, he became overwhelmed by all his emotions. He also said that he had become depressed over the last year. Adam told me that the only activity which distracted him from his depression was playing video games. Adam told me that he did not really want to upset his parents, but he was not motivated to do his school work, even on the days when his parents relented and allowed him to stay home from school. He admitted that he was being annoyed by the constant attention from his parents. Adam, like every other adolescent I have ever seen in therapy, just wanted to do what he wanted to do without being 'hassled' by his parents.

Adam's parents informed me that when Adam did not want to go to school, he would have an intense emotional meltdown. This meltdown included his emphatic begging to not have to go to school along with his screaming and crying. Because of the mother's label of mild autism and his recent behavior, his mother and father were very concerned that Adam would be unable to assume responsibility for his life. The thoughts of Adam unable to support himself or to control his emotions caused them much worry and led to their overcompensation of attention on Adam. The mother, in particular, constantly monitored him, even when he was behaving 'normally.' While Adam's mother loved him dearly, she did acknowledge that her anxiety about Adam's well-being had grown over the past two years.

Adam's father worked long hours at an automotive facility and was not around very much. He had relied on his wife's advice on how to deal with Adam. The father informed me that he was the one family member who stayed positive and upbeat for everyone else. He worked hard to help his wife who was obviously very stressed by the whole situation. He smiled often during the intake session and he seemed very intent on doing whatever was asked of him if it would help his son. Adam's parents were both genuinely concerned and wanted the best for him, but Adam's emotional outbursts and depression were a battle they faced weekly. They were both overly anxious about Adam's mental health, and adolescent Adam was frustrated by his parents' actions and their attempts at discipline.

From a linear perspective, it is easy to pick a cause (A) to this effect (B):

A (cause): Adam's behavior –> B (effect): family turmoil

In this case, the therapist could simply use interventions to adjust Adam's thoughts and behaviors which hopefully would restore harmony to the household. However, we cannot be sure that only one 'part' of the situation is the single cause. On the other hand, perhaps the mother's constant monitoring and micromanaging creates the outbursts and depression in Adam? Or perhaps it is the busy father's lack of involvement in the family that motivates Adam to resort to drastic measures to get his father's attention? Or perhaps the father's lack of interaction with the mother causes issues within the household and Adam's behavior is an unconscious expression of his parents' marital struggles?

Again, if the therapist only focuses on one 'part,' then the other parts may continue to make change elusive. As in our previous example, this bus does not run for reasons other than a lack of gas. Rather than focusing on the problem which brought the family for help, I adopted a nonlinear perspective in this case. Struggling with Adam about his behaviors, convincing his mother to stop managing her son, or motivating his father to spend more time with the family were all good and helpful options, but each option ignored the patterns which connected them.

After spending a half hour with the family discussing the 'problem' of Adam's behavior, I dismissed Adam from the room and talked privately with his parents. I suggested that the way to help Adam was for him to find a way to experience a feeling of 'helpfulness' in the family. Utilizing their concerns about Adam, I explained to the parents that because of Adam's struggles, he did not have sufficient opportunities to help others. I acknowledged their concerns about his possible autism and his depression, but I said that I believed that Adam feeling 'helpful' would be a good way to combat these issues.

Knowing the answer to my question, I still inquired which person in the family was the happiest and most optimistic. Both parents quickly answered that it was the father. Adam's mother earnestly referred to him as the 'positive cheerleader in the home.' I then directed that, when he was at home with his family, the father was to pretend for the next two weeks that he was deeply depressed. I explained that in this short time period if Adam helped his father, Adam would have a better sense of self-esteem. I told the parents that this experience would help his depression and anxiety about school. I asked Adam's mother to go along with her husband's depressed person performance and, over the next two weeks, to frequently express her concern about her husband's condition to Adam. I instructed them that there must be absolutely no discussion of Adam's problem. The only focus should be on the father's 'depression.'

Adam was brought back into the room and we all adopted a somber state as I told Adam that a family secret had been uncovered in our therapy. This secret was that his positive, optimistic father had, in reality, been suffering from depression for a long time and he had been hiding it from his family. I encouraged Adam and his mother to direct all their energy into helping the father feel better while trying not to worry too much about him. I have to admit, Adam's father put on an Academy Award worthy performance in my office when we unmasked the 'secret' of his depression. The family quietly left and were scheduled to be seen in two weeks for the purpose of checking on the father's 'depression.'

When the family returned to therapy, the parents reported that Adam had been very helpful to his father over the last two weeks. He had also started helping his mother more often around the home. Adam had only twice refused to go to school instead of having the daily emotional outbursts. In fact, according to his mother, Adam's emotional reaction during those two outbursts was much more subdued than usual. The father, with a wink, said he was feeling much better about his depression. The mother reported that she experienced overall fewer problems with Adam. I thanked Adam for helping his father during the tough time, but I also warned the family not to consider the father cured of his depression since sometimes the symptoms take a long time to disappear. In time, Adam became less emotional about school and his mother learned to decrease her managing of him. Adam and his father also grew closer.

Even though client change can happen in a linear way, are we truly able to fit human behavior into a simple cause and effect no-fail process? The lure of the simplistic one solution for all problems type of therapy often neglects the reality of an alive human organism. By opening our minds to a nonlinear way of performing psychotherapy, we have a more holistic view of generative change. This perception of therapy requires more creativity and more curiosity on the part of the therapist, which can make therapy, not only effective, but transformational.

CHAPTER 7

THE MAGIC OF RITUAL

The use of rituals can create magical experiences. Every culture has created rituals to aid in life transitions. Familiar rituals such as weddings, funerals, bar mitzvahs, and graduations serve as a psychological connection to the different stages of life that we move through. Ceremonial and healing rituals are used to facilitate curative actions in order to alleviate emotional suffering. These rituals are intensive and transforming experiences that are symbolic in nature. Rituals usually are metaphoric since they operate outside the usual, the rational, and the analytical means of knowledge. These tasks usually involve unique imagery and multiple sensory experiences which activates unconscious processes in the clients' inner world.

Rituals for transformation and healing have been used for thousands of years. As far back as the Neolithic period of human development, rituals were used to help people on an inner journey to find their way to their destination. In ancient Egypt and Greece, rituals were used to change people's consciousness and to alter the life patterns of those who participated. These practices, which were often held in secret, were considered crucial for one's personal development. Healing rituals historically have been used to help people move from one stage of their lives onto the next stage. According to Campbell and Moyers (1988), rituals 'have to do with your recognition of the new role you are in, the process of throwing off the old one and coming out in the new' (p. 14).

The use of rituals in Western culture is negligible in comparison with many other cultures. For the most part, rituals are little used since our culture places little value in them. I think this is a tremendous mistake because rituals can open up worlds to us that our ordinary perceptions cannot achieve. According to Hinton and Kirmayer (2017), 'healing rituals shift sufferers' mode of being-in-the-world, including their cognitive, emotional, and physical state or stance, toward openness to new ways of being' (p. 4). Rituals involve a shift in a person's emotional state which can have long-term positive effects.

The perception that the psychotherapy process itself is a therapeutic ritual is not a new idea. Some researchers viewed the psychotherapist in the role of the director of the ritual who provided their clients with a distinct space for transformation (Cole, 2003; Moore, 1983; Usandivaras, 1985; Wyrostock, 1995). Traditionally, the primary and often used tool of psychotherapy has been conversation. This interaction has been seen as the predominant method of creating change in clients, but conversation in therapy is primarily a conscious activity. However, focusing strictly on conscious conversation may be limiting since words are quite often insufficient to adequately express the negative, embodied experiences from which clients seek refuge. The use of certain symbolic ritual actions has the power to move clients to a space where language is not necessary for change. The willingness to introduce ritual actions into therapy creates a transformative atmosphere where clients are taken out of their ordinary perceptions and ordinary responses.

Therapeutic rituals may be thought of as symbolic modes of communication acted out in a specific order. Van der Hart (1983) defined rituals as 'prescribed symbolic acts that must be performed in a certain way and in a certain order, and may or may not be accompanied by verbal formulas' (p. 5). These symbolic acts can provide clients with a new way to alter their relationships and their habitual ways of interaction. Therapeutic rituals create new meanings to situations that clients have experienced. Rituals can also allow clients to experience their situations in a different context. Therapeutic rituals are experiential processes in which clients may construct new beginnings, while ending their old limiting patterns, and connecting to their own emotions and thoughts in a safe manner. Cole (2003) views therapeutic rituals as 'a structured set of actions developed collaboratively by the therapist and client to effect a transition from one psychological state to another' (p. 184).

Therapeutic rituals differ from the usual skill-building exercises in therapy homework since they use symbols with unconscious connotations. Symbols are the foundation of rituals because these symbols hold multiple meanings for clients. These meanings have significance for clients that words alone might not be able to acquire. Rituals can create new understandings and new perspectives for clients which exist at the nonverbal level. They can also help to break through rigid and ineffective patterns since the ritual can give clients an out of the ordinary experience. Having clients perform therapeutic rituals can also provide a change in the structure of their relationships in other aspects of their lives (Van der Hart, 1983). Therapy sessions generally take on a different look and feel when rituals are introduced, and if properly implemented, they can generate a session which feels magical to both the therapist and the client.

Engaging clients in ritual activities allows them to be aware that something 'is' different. There is no intellectualizing that something 'could' be different. The ritual does more than merely provide clients with a task; it creates a feeling of the connection of the self to something far greater and more mysterious. Rituals are a means to take clients out of their usual routine and immerse them in a novel experience. This experience must be emotionally compelling in order to engage clients in a multiple sensory situation and allow for the discovery of abilities which they have yet to realize. As Kirmayer (1999) points out, the 'manipulation of symbols through imaginal dialog and ritual enactments can reorganize cognitive schemas, unconscious dynamics and interpersonal interaction' (p. 451).

Rituals will increase the intensity of an experience when they are filled with the dramatic and with sensory and emotional involvement. If they permeate the emotional core of clients, there are usually lasting effects. These transforming kinds of experiences are difficult to have in the verbally oriented and lower intensity nature of most psychotherapy (Goodwyn, 2016). Rituals also cause a neurobiological shift in how clients perceive their own personal issues. As Hogue (2006) states, 'Ritual participation is believed to engage the autonomic nervous system, frequently alternating between the sympathetic and parasympathetic subsystems. These processes then arouse or quiet subcortical neural processing and hormonal involvement, resulting in emotional engagement' (p. 231). The inclusion of spiritual elements into rituals for some clients can cause a sensation of a connection with the mysterious and unknown (Cole, 2003).

Rituals can also bring out new client narratives. Having clients perform unique and unusual tasks can shift their perceptions away from the fixed left-brained oriented analytical response to a focus on right-brain symbolism. The enacting of an intense ritual also has the power to adjust how clients emotionally respond to older memories, as 'the self-conscious attention that is focused on both narrative and ritual performance undoubtedly creates a constellation of circumstances in which memories may be recalled and re-encoded' (Hogue, 2006, p. 233). Cole (2003) has suggested that rituals help to reach deeper psychological structures which can create a lasting memory at the unconscious level in the clients' psyche.

When rituals are used in therapy, they provide a process of reconstructing and rebuilding disruptions in the clients' past. An effective healing ritual will activate multiple experiences and can support life transitions in clients. Imber-Black (2003) believes therapeutic rituals for healing must have three primary elements. The first is the 'affective' element, which recognizes the clients' emotional and physical pain and a sense of loss. The second is the 'cognitive' element, which alternates between the clients being able to let go of pain and their ability to hold on to stability. The third is the 'behavior' element, which is the symbolic act of completion. When all of these elements are present in a ritual, clients may have a deeper sense of finality in their responses to their problems. It may also provide a gateway and a path for moving forward in their lives.

Therapeutic rituals can connect clients to situations or to people with whom they have lost a connection. Having clients recall an activity they enjoyed prior to a disruption or a trauma in their lives can help them to realize that they still have important resources useful in moving forward. If clients are unable to remember a useful activity, then designing a new healthy activity will give them the feeling of being more in control of their lives. They become more open to new possibilities.

Rituals which involve the letting go of past pain are not uncommon in psychotherapy. These rituals are a cleansing process which has the purpose of releasing clients from their emotional burdens. It helps clients to move beyond the grieving process. These rituals may take the form of the client writing letters to those who have harmed them and then burning or burying the letters. Any symbolic item, such as photographs, jewelry, and so on, can be used in the letting go ritual (Imber-Black, 2003).

I once worked with a client named Denise who had been shot in the leg by a stray bullet from the gun of a gang member embroiled in a fight with a member of a rival gang. Denise had been simply standing across the street waiting for a bus when the fight broke out. She came to therapy because of her recurring dreams about the shooting, as well as her overall fear of being out in public. Fortunately, Denise had minimal injury as a result of the shooting which only required stiches. However, despite her good fortune in the physical realm, her psychological state had been severely affected by the shooting.

On the first day of our session, Denise presented me with a plastic bag containing the pair of jeans that she had been wearing when she was shot. The jeans were covered in dried blood and had been ripped by the bullet and the resulting medical care. She told me that she had brought her jeans with her so that I could fully understand the impact that this event had had on her. Denise said that she was a prisoner of her memories of the shooting, but she desperately wanted to move past the event and to reclaim her life. She also told me that she now was worrying more than ever about death.

Since she had brought her jeans to therapy, I decided that we could use them as a part of a ritual action to help Denise move forward. I asked Denise if she would be willing to have a funeral for her jeans. Denise was not sure that she understood what I was asking. I explained to her that holding on to the jeans could be a reason why she continuously played out the shooting in her mind. I told her that a funeral for the jeans could be a signal to her unconscious mind that she was now ready to let go of her fear and the associated fearful memories. Denise accepted the idea and we scheduled a funeral for the next session.

When Denise arrived for the next session, the lights in my office were lowered in a subdued fashion, and flowers had been placed around the room. I laid her jeans on a small table in the middle of the room and placed a white cloth over them. Denise could not help smiling at the whole idea and she let me know that it was certainly an odd thing to do. We both said a few words in a playfully somber tone about how much the jeans had meant to Denise and how we both appreciated all they had done for her. We expressed a sadness that the jeans would have to be disposed of, in spite of the wonderful benefits they had provided to Denise.

As we were about to close our funeral, Denise began to cry openly. She said that she hated to see her jeans go and felt they were taken away from her by cruel chance. Through her tears, she talked about what it was like to know that she would never again have that pair of jeans and how it made her sad. Even though she was supposedly talking about her bloodied and torn jeans, we both knew she was really talking about the personal loss of a sense of safety in her world. When she grew silent, I placed the jeans in a black bag and stepped out of the room to dispose of them. In the next session, Denise told me that she had less fear and that her fearful dreams were not as frequent. She also found that she was able to use some of the cognitive restructuring exercises we had explored in our first session more effectively.

Like Denise, I too had a moving encounter in a 'letting go' ritual in my role, not as a therapist but as a client. I had been seeing my own therapist, Sue, for months as I navigated the after-effects of a divorce that I had not wanted. I had become depressed and felt deeply, emotionally wounded by the situation. In spite of all the excellent therapy Sue had provided as I dealt with my life changes, we both agreed that I was a bit stuck in my grief over the divorce. Consciously, I wanted to move on with my life, but I was unable to move forward even when I detected and disputed my own limiting internal dialogue or when I fully expressed my emotions about the situation. I was entangled by the past and just could not find a way to break free.

At one of my sessions, Sue brought in a large silver helium balloon. She handed me the balloon and a black marker. She directed me to write down on one side of the silver balloon all the things I missed about my marriage. Sue sat quietly as I wrote all I could and completely filled up one side of the balloon. She then told me to turn the balloon over and write down all the things I would not miss in my marriage. I again followed the directive and filled up the other side of the balloon with writing.

When I completed the task, Sue escorted me and the balloon to the very top of her two-story office building. She instructed me to read again both sides of the balloon and then to release it into the sky when I was ready to let go. To be honest, my logical brain thought the activity was a bit silly, until I let the balloon go. As we watched it go higher and higher in the air, I began to feel a stirring of emotion in my chest as the balloon disappeared into the clouds. I found that I was feeling an odd mixture of grief and relief at the same time. Sue gave me a hug and announced that our session was now over.

On the drive home from my session, I suddenly began to feel tears flow down my cheeks as the memory of that balloon floating into the heavens hit me. I began to feel a shift within myself as I pulled the car over to the side of the road and finally allowed myself to cry. It felt as if my heart opened and all the bad feelings that I had been wrestling with for months decided to come out. After only a few minutes of emotional distress, a feeling of peace began to envelop me. From that point on, I was able to begin moving forward in my life. I credit the simple ritual of the letting go of that helium balloon with initiating my healing.

Rituals help us move beyond the use of intellectual insight alone, which may not be effective in changing our clients' perceptions and actions. Too often clients remain stuck in their problem despite our extensive clinical work on their cognitions. In addition to traditional therapy work, if we give clients some unique, strange, and mysterious experiences, then this often helps them become more flexible in how they deal with their problem or situation. This may be due to how the unique experience is registered in the client's emotional brain, sometimes referred to as the unconscious mind. There are still many therapists who operate out of the paradigm that if clients can consciously 'understand' their problems, then they can rationally solve those problems. This paradigm can sometimes work very well, however, there are also clients who remain stuck in a loop of rumination with no a way out of the loop. The introduction of a ritual into therapy can be a way for the emotional brain to finally get out of the loop.

I discovered that the designing and implementing of unconscious symbolic tasks for clients helped them find a way out of their rumination loop. Ritual tasks bypass the rational mind and instead go to the heart of the unconscious mind, which takes in information through symbolic means. These tasks represent the clients' problems (as well as the solutions) to their unconscious minds. The goal of using these rituals is first to express the problem and second to find a solution in a metaphoric way. The task can be experienced either inside or outside of the therapy room. Rituals allow clients to integrate the healing experiences in a way that is unique to them. These rituals provide clients with more flexibility and more access to their own inner resources when working through the issue being faced. The use of strange tasks in therapy may sound a little ridiculous to our regimented, linear thinking, but to our nonlinear, unconscious mind, these rituals can be a gateway to different healing experiences.

In my study and exploration of other healing traditions, I have found that it is not uncommon for healing practitioners to request their clients to perform tasks which are out of the ordinary, but which represent the inner struggles the clients are presently experiencing in their lives. These ritual tasks given to clients are beyond the realm of left-brained language and reason, but, instead, they operate purely on a right-brain symbolic level. For instance, I once heard about a Mexican Curandero, what we might call a shaman or native healer, who worked with a woman suffering from intense emotional turmoil. The woman's source of her emotional problems appeared to the Curandero to be related to the negative childhood issues which the woman had with her mother.

The Curandero directed the woman to buy a large watermelon and to tape a picture of her mother on it. She was then to carry the watermelon on a long, arduous hike through the mountains. At the end of her hike, she was then directed to look at the picture of her mother for a long period of time and then smash the watermelon. The woman was then to bury the watermelon and to write her mother a letter telling her how much she appreciated the good things her mother had done. When the woman followed through on the Curandero's directives, she found that she was no longer in as much turmoil about the childhood issues with her mother. It appeared that the symbolic task initiated clearing up the old emotional wounds that had persisted for many years. The symbolic nature of the ritual allowed the woman to put down the heavy watermelon (which was symbolic of the emotional burden she had been carrying) after the long, tiring effort of the mountain hike (which was symbolic of the previous years of her life) and then to destroy the watermelon (the burden and connection to her painful past) to reclaim her own power.

It is important that, in order for the ritual to be fully effective, therapists must build an expectancy in clients that something miraculous will occur after the ritual is fully completed. Expectation can have a remarkable effect on positive outcomes in therapy. If clients accept the idea that the therapist truly believes that a ritual will help them, they are not only more inclined to perform the ritual, but they also will expect to see changes resulting from the task. It is not always essential for clients to know what they will experience as a result of the ritual, but only that they believe that something of special importance can happen to them. Not revealing the purpose of the task builds curiosity and expectation on the part of clients. The very act of persuading clients to perform a ritual is in itself a means for clients to do something completely different. Just performing an out of the ordinary activity can break entrenched patterns. If proper expectancy is built by the therapist, clients are often more engaged in the completion of the act, even when there is no specific conscious goal.

Van der Hart (1983) makes a distinction between rituals designed on the spot in a creative and spontaneous manner as 'open,' and those which have more specifics, structure, and forethought as 'closed.' Open rituals may suddenly appear in the improvisational exchange between the therapists and the clients. They may suddenly occur and break any momentary therapeutic impasse. Closed rituals may have specific set time periods, specific people or objects involved, and specific locations involved in their implementation. Either of these can be performed within or outside the therapy session. 'In session' rituals can be effective since clients can experience a difference in their emotional states while in a safe location. In these office-bound rituals, therapists are the directors of the ritual and can ensure that the clients fully understand the process. The therapists' presence can also be helpful as a witness to the event or to supply enhancement for any dramatic aspect of the performance (Imber-Black, 2003).

When matching a symbol to a specific ritual, it is important that we carefully listen to the clients' choice of words and phrases used when discussing their problem. Sometimes it is helpful to seek input from clients on what symbols might work for them. This inclusion of clients' ideas can help the therapy process as,

> Client generated symbols tend to foster a co-investment in the thera-
> peutic process. Because of the symbolic nature of the ritual, the actor
> is bound to the interaction. This action is change-oriented and because
> the level of emotional intensity that can occur, the client co-investment
> in their therapeutic progress is further encouraged. This co-invest-
> ment can result in clients continuing to work on their issues between
> sessions.
>
> *(Winek & Craven, 2003, p. 256)*

I have found the following common structure for designing ritual tasks useful. This structure can be used for a variety of problems with which clients are experiencing.

1) Pay attention to the metaphors that clients use to describe their problem.

In conversation, clients will give therapists certain metaphors and analogies for their problems in the conversation without realizing it. A therapist may hear a client say that she feels 'stuck between a rock and a hard place.' This kind of phrase gives clues about how clients symbolically represent their problems to themselves. When a ritual makes use of elements in clients' metaphors, clients unconsciously connect to the ritual at a deeper level than their logical mind, which had been trying to solve the problem.

2) Envision how the problem can be solved in a symbolic act.

Allow your intuition to come up with a means of using the client metaphors in some specific action that clients will have to perform. Assign a symbol to the metaphor. If a client says she is feeling 'stuck between a rock and a hard place,' then she could be directed to buy a sledgehammer and some cement blocks. The problem could be painted in dark colors on the blocks. The client using the sledgehammer, breaks the blocks. This symbolic act lets her know that she can always break out of her place 'between a rock and a hard place.'

3) Have clients do something that is an out of the ordinary action in order to interrupt their unconscious patterns.

This example of using a sledgehammer to break out of her problem must be something that this woman has never done previously or the novelty of the event loses its impact. If she were a construction worker who broke up cement every day, this action would not be a wise choice. Humans are creatures of habit, doing the same thing every day the same way. In order to have an impact on clients, rituals must have an element of novelty and mystery attached to the task.

4) Make the task something that requires some effort.

It is important that there is some effort on the part of the clients for they will not experience anything of significance without effort. This does not mean that the task has to be excessively physically difficult, but it can require clients to exert some emotional, mental, intellectual, and/or physical power in order to complete the ritual. At the same time, the task must not be completely overwhelming. If the ritual requires more effort than the client possesses, then most clients will not do it. As Jodorowsky (2015) recommends for the creation of rituals in his shamanic psychotherapy work he calls 'Psychomagic,' 'To heal or solve a problem, we need an iron will. To not do what we desire to do or to not do what we do not desire to do causes us a deep lack of self-esteem, which causes depression and serious illnesses. The tireless battle to fulfill a goal that seems impossible develops our vital energy' (p. 7). Certainly, in our example, breaking up cement blocks requires effort for someone who has never had that experience.

Let us examine how this ritual structure would work using one of my cases:

> A woman named Annie came to me for therapy because of the overwhelming apprehension that she experienced when she had to deal with her mother. Annie explained that since she was a small child, her mother had a mean-spirited habit of verbally shutting Annie down. Growing up, Annie learned to say no more than she needed to because her mother would see to it that Annie was verbally overpowered until she submitted to her mother's will. Her mother was extremely argumentative and always had to be right no matter what topic was being discussed (even when it was obvious to everyone else that her mother was wrong).

To the present day, Annie's talks with her mother were often contentious and anxiety provoking for her. Now, as an adult, Annie tried to avoid interactions with her mother because of her anxiety about her mother's arguing and shutting her down. She told me that she felt 'being emotionally choked' by her mother's ability to verbally cut her down. Annie believed that she had little ability to feel anything other than anxiety when dealing with her quarrelsome mother.

I directed Annie to bring a doll from home or buy one at a store and bring it into her next session. When she arrived for the next session, Annie brought a doll her mother had given her many years ago when she was a child. Strangely enough, the doll resembled the way the adult Annie looked. I gave Annie a roll of twine. I and asked her to tie it very tightly around the doll, from its neck to its feet. I told her that the twine should be so tight that it could not be removed without cutting it. I also told Annie that she needed to make extra tight knots around the doll's throat area. When she had finished tying up the doll, I then told her she now had to remove the twine, but she could not use scissors. She had to somehow loosen the very tight knots she had just tied around the doll without using anything to cut the twine.

Annie struggled and struggled to remove the twine. After about ten minutes she was able to remove the twine from the doll. I then told her that she was to take the doll back home and to hide it in her closet for two days. After that time, she was to bring the doll out of the closet and to put it in a place where she kept her family photos. At our next session, Annie said to me that she had followed the directives and had noticed she no longer was quite as worried and apprehensive about talking to her mother. She believed that she had reduced her anxiety by close to 50 percent. Annie still did not fully understand why tying up the doll would have had an impact on her, but she was very happy with the result of the experiment.

This task followed the structure of ritual previously given:

1) Pay attention to the metaphors that clients use to describe their problem.

   Annie clearly stated that she felt as if she were being emotionally choked. The metaphor of being choked is a powerful image that mirrors Annie's long term real life struggle with her mother.

2) Envision how the problem can be solved in a symbolic act.

   The tying of the twine around the doll, specifically the throat area, acted as a symbol of her experience. The use of a doll harkens Annie's mind back to her childhood experiences.

3) Have clients do something that is out of the ordinary action in order to interrupt their unconscious patterns.

   Adults rarely tie up dolls with twine. In Annie's case, she had never previously done anything like this action. Her unconscious thought patterns of being 'choked' and 'shut down' were represented by the doll restricted by twine.

4) Make the task something that requires some effort.

   After Annie took a lot of care to tie the knots securely, they were difficult to untie, and she had to struggle with freeing the doll from its restrictions. This is a way for Annie's emotional brain to understand the idea that, since she is now an adult, Annie can free herself at any time from her mother's restrictive behavior.

Conducting therapeutic rituals also helps clients to symbolically face certain situations or certain people that they have avoided. This inability to confront may be due to geographic restrictions, people are not available or are now deceased, or the clients just feel overwhelmed by the conscious action of facing what they fear. Instead, rituals allow clients to have a symbolic experience of success in situations which they felt ill-prepared. The symbolic nature of the ritual gives the clients' conscious mind security and safety, while at the same time, giving their emotional brain an experience representative of a real event.

I once worked with a man named Henry who came to therapy because of his high levels of anxiety. Henry had traced the cause of his anxiety back to when he was a young child between seven and ten years old. Henry recounted that he had been severely abused by his stepmother. Along with the physical abuse, his stepmother had also engaged in psychological abuse by performing, what Henry described as 'evil spells.' Henry recounted the terror of being forced into certain rituals which were designed to summon forth the power of evil in order to harm people against whom his stepmother held grudges. Henry detailed how he was forced to stand in a dark room in the middle of a circle made of candles while his stepmother walked around the circle loudly chanting in a frightening language that he did not understand. He was always threatened by his stepmother at the end of the rituals saying that he had better not tell his father. Henry's father was frequently away on business and knew nothing about these activities or the abuse. Henry was repeatedly told by his stepmother that he would receive a horrible demise at the hand of demonic forces if he shared her activities with anyone.

Eventually, his father found out about the abuse and about the strange activities of Henry's stepmother and removed her from the home. Even though his father quickly divorced his stepmother, Henry still lived in terror that she would return to wreak havoc and obtain revenge against Henry and his father. Of course, over time, Henry's fears waned, but they were always in the back of his mind. Henry was a rational thinker, but he found that as he aged he continued to feel a more intense sense of fear about his stepmother. Even though Henry had not seen her in over 30 years and had moved to the other side of the country, he still had recurring nightmares about being captured by her and having to submit to her cruel rituals. He found himself looking over his shoulder when he was out in public and felt concerned that she could be watching him. He also had a fear of the dark that persisted as he aged. He recounted his nightly ritual of triple checking all locks while also making sure that every room had a nightlight that was working. It seemed that the bulk of Henry's life was centered on his fear of his vindictive, spell performing former stepmother.

In my office, Henry admitted that he was embarrassed that he still was living in fear. He also believed that this fear had often caused problems in his romantic relationships since he felt he could never fully trust any woman. His own mother had died when he was four years old, and he said that he had very few memories of her. Henry felt trapped in his irrational fear. He openly wondered if perhaps his stepmother had indeed spellbound him to live in fear. He found this a plausible possibility because of his first-hand knowledge of his stepmother's desire to cause evil and despair in other people's lives. Henry told me that if he could just be released from the spell he was under, he believed his life would be pleasant. He was succeeding in other areas of his life, particularly in his work, but he knew that he could not be happy until he was able to get beyond the fears rooted in his early childhood.

I empathized with Henry and his plight. I told him that his situation was a unique one, but it was also one which he could change. Henry appeared to visibly relax when I told him that there was a way out of this terror. I asked Henry if he would be willing to come back to see me within a week so that we could do something radical to stop the torment of his fear. Henry quickly agreed. As he was leaving my office, I told Henry that our next session would be a very different session. He was to mentally prepare himself to move beyond his former stepmother's psychic grip on him. I directed him to shower and shave before coming to the next session. I also asked him to wear the color white since this is the color of purity. Henry seemed a little confused by my request, but he gamely agreed to follow it none the less.

Henry showed up for his next session the following week clean, neat, and freshly shaved wearing a bright white t-shirt and a pair of white slacks. He appeared a little apprehensive of what might transpire in our session, but I could sense there was also a positive expectancy in him. Henry was extremely wary of his fear and was ready to change. He told me as we sat down that he was afraid about what was going to happen next, but he was hopeful that his emotional pain would finally end. I commended Henry's bravery and his desire to take charge of his own life. I also told him that I was very confident that some change was going to happen, even though I was not sure exactly what that change would be.

I pulled out a sheet of white paper and gave it to Henry. I asked him to write out in detail every bad thing his former stepmother had ever done to him. I wanted him to go into as much graphic description as he could and to take all the time he needed. Henry obliged and needed two more sheets of paper to complete his task. I could see the fear in his eyes as he wrote down the stories of his abuse at the hands of his stepmother. He wrote for quite a while in silence. After nearly 30 minutes of writing, he presented me with his sheets of white paper filled with the horrific activities that no child should ever have to endure.

I looked over the sheets of paper and then asked him to read them aloud. I told him to read them to me as if it were the last time he was ever going to read and hear these stories of his troubled young life. Henry read the stories back to me, but with much apprehension. He stopped a few times to compose himself as the stories were clearly very difficult for him to relive. When he had finished reading, I again told him how much I admired his bravery and his courage to face the unpleasant experiences in his life. Henry seemed relieved to at last be done reading his stories.

At that point, I told Henry that I had something for him. I left the room for a couple of moments and returned with a 'spirit board.' A spirit board is a thin, flat board which has the letters of the alphabet, the numbers zero to nine, and different words written on it. It is commonly known as a tool used by people who believe in spirits to contact the dead and a variety of disembodied specters. When Henry saw the board, he had a visceral and negative reaction and asked me why I had brought the board into the room. I asked him if he knew what it was. He quickly told me that his stepmother used the spirit board to talk to evil spirits to persuade them to do her bidding. Henry nervously laughed when he told me about his stepmother's use of the board.

I explained to Henry that in order to break the spell that his time with his stepmother had created, he had to unconsciously disrupt its hold on him. The spirit board was a symbol of his stepmother and he was going to finally break free of her psychic clutches. I handed the board to him which he reluctantly took. I asked him to focus his eyes on the board and remember anything about his former stepmother that came into his mind. After a moment or two of Henry staring uncomfortably at the spirit board, I handed him a roll of tape. He was to tape the sheets of paper, which he had written all the frightening and horrible things his stepmother had done, to the spirit board.

When Henry had finished taping the papers to the board, I then took him outside of the office. We went to an area where there were many trees to ensure our privacy. I told Henry that to be free of his former stepmother, he had to destroy the spirit board. I explained that this action would create a break in the connection that his unconscious mind still had with his stepmother. I told him that he was to immediately destroy the board using whatever means he saw fit. I let him know that I would not help him to do it. I told him that it would be difficult to destroy the board by himself, but I knew he could do it. For a few moments, Henry looked at the board which had been placed on the ground and appeared unsure of how to proceed. He just stared at the board and stood motionless.

All of a sudden, Henry began to stomp on the spirit board. He then picked it up and started hitting it against a tree, but the board stayed intact. He then placed the board at an angle against a tree and jumped on it using his entire body weight. With a crack, the board came apart. Henry took each one of the cracked pieces and used the same maneuver to splinter and crack all of them. Within a couple of minutes, the spirit board had been totally and completely destroyed.

I picked up the pieces, placed them in a plastic bag which I had brought with me, and handed the bag with the splintered and broken pieces of the spirit board to Henry. I told him that he should take the remnants of the board home, build a small fire, and throw them into it. Henry was then to take the ashes from the fire and use it as fertilizer for a new plant which he was to put in his yard. He was free to pick any plant he wanted as long as it represented a sense of renewal to him. I then dismissed Henry and told him I would see him in two weeks.

When Henry arrived at his next session, I was instantly aware that he was more relaxed than our previous time together. He informed me that, after he had burned the remnants of the spirit board and buried them under a pretty plant, he noticed a reduction in his fear. He also noticed that his body felt a little lighter than it had felt before. Henry also said that even though he still had some fear, he felt more in control of his fear than he had in many years. He had decided that he would turn off one of the nightlights in a room he rarely went into. He felt safe with no lighting in it. Henry commented that he found that he was not looking over his shoulder as much as he had previously.

In time, Henry began to make peace with his troubled past. He would eventually turn off more of the nightlights in his house (although he continued to have one in his bedroom). Henry tried his hand at dating again since he believed he was in a better place to begin trusting women. It was still an ongoing process, but he believed that he was making progress. One day he told me that he had gone to his local bookstore and had intentionally walked down the aisle that contained books on witchcraft and related subjects. Henry noticed that, while he did not like the topics in any way, he did not feel the fear or the repulsion he once felt before he destroyed the spirit board. It appeared that the ritual of destroying the board had indeed freed Henry from the psychological ties with his former stepmother. He still had more therapy work to do, but he also had a new sense of freedom in which to do the work.

Sometimes, rituals can be more effective if they are performed outside rather than inside the therapy room. This gives clients a sense of privacy as they perform the requested tasks. Without the pressure of time, out of session rituals can be longer and more elaborate tasks, taking days or even weeks to complete. Out of session rituals can be tasks which the client does only one time or multiple times a day during a specified time period. These out of session tasks have the advantage of pulling in more resources to be used in the ritual rather than using only what resources are available in the therapy room.

An example of an out of session ritual involved the couple, Amber and Mike, who were on the verge of divorce. In their first session, they unveiled their problems which included Mike's binge drinking and Amber's accompanying enabling behavior. They had been married only a few years, but Mike's nightly beer drinking and intoxication had become an issue. This caused a chain of events that included arguing, Amber's threats of leaving, and Mike's apologizing and promising to stop his drinking, which never happened. Mike was not fully committed to the idea of giving up his beer. He believed that he did not have a real problem because he was able to hold down a good job and to provide for his family. He said he had no history of any legal troubles due to his drinking and believed he was capable of controlling it; he just chose not to do so.

Amber felt trapped in Mike's cycle of binge drinking, yet she had enabled it to continue by relenting to Mike's promise that he would cut back on drinking. His promises to stop drinking came about when Amber threatened to leave him. Up until two weeks ago, she had no real intention to leave Mike, but a recent bad experience with Mike's drunkenness in front of her two small children had pushed her over the edge. She packed up her clothes, took the children, and left to stay with her mother for the past two weeks. Amber's departure had shook Mike to his core. He was desperately afraid that she would divorce him and he was now motivated to come to therapy to get her back. However, at the same time, Mike was still enjoying his nightly beer.

It was very apparent to me that Amber and Mike did indeed love each other very much, but they were hopelessly stuck in a pattern of his drinking, her enabling, and the chaos which resulted. I intuitively knew that any real discussion about Mike's drinking would cause him to shut down, feel that he was being ganged up on, and made to be the 'bad guy.' I also knew that, even though Amber wanted him to stop drinking, her constant micro-managing of Mike had heavily contributed to the marital discontent and maybe even gave Mike an excuse to continue drinking.

In our session, Mike told me how he wanted Amber to come back home. He disclosed that he always worried about being alone since his father had left his mother when Mike was only six years old. He told me that he had tried for 30 years to connect with his father, but he had little success. He finally realized that his father had no interest in Mike nor Mike's children. This emotional wound had plagued Mike for most of his life. He attempted to get approval from his father, but it always ended in disappointment for Mike. Since his mother had passed away, Mike clearly was afraid of losing Amber because she was the one person he felt he did have some connection. He also was afraid that his children would feel the pain of abandonment as he had felt from his father if Amber divorced him. In spite of Mike's bravado when he began the session, his disclosure of his painful past reduced him to tears.

Amber informed me that her father had been an alcoholic, and she was fully aware that she was in the same enabling patterns with Mike that she had witnessed in her mother. She intellectually knew that she was part of the problem, yet she was so deeply entrenched in her pattern of behavior that she was afraid that she could not stop. She wanted a home life that was better for her children than her own childhood. Her memories of her father's drunken rants and his falling asleep at the dinner table were not pleasant and were embarrassing to her. Even though she had loved her father, who had passed away several years earlier, she admitted she had few positive memories of being with him.

I told Amber and Mike that I clearly recognized the deep love that they had for each other. They both visibly relaxed as my comment seemed to validate the importance of their relationship to them. I then told them that their relationship was being overshadowed by the 'ghosts of the fathers.' The behavior of their fathers had colored the way each of them related to the other. I acknowledged both of their concerns about the others' behavior and complimented them on sticking in the marriage as long as they had. I told them they obviously had an enormous dedication to each other, even if it did not appear that way at the moment.

Amber and Mike needed to have an experience together that was radically different from their nightly arguments about Mike's drinking. I had to give them an activity that would generate a change in the way they perceived their problem. Any direct discussion about Mike's drinking or Amber's enabling would have limited results since this line of discussion was a nightly occurrence for them. Something that interrupted their usual patterns, even for just one night, was needed.

I asked Amber if she would be willing to move back home for just a couple of nights. She agreed. I then asked if they were truly committed to changing this situation. They both said that they were indeed committed. After obtaining their commitment, I told them that I had something very out of the ordinary for them to do. In order for them to move forward in their marriage in a positive way, they would have to do something very strange. I told them that what I was going to ask them to do was something that they had never before been asked to do. I informed them that their commitment to this task could be taken as a clear sign to each other of their commitment to their marriage. They were both intrigued about what I was going to ask them to do.

I sat quietly for a moment in order to build anticipation for what I was going to say. I then told them that after dinner one night to use a cloth to wash their dishes. They were to wash the dishes together and then wring out the water from the cloth when they were finished. They were to leave the dishcloth lying out on the kitchen counter for three days. The dishcloth was not to be touched or used during that time. After three days, they were to take the sour-smelling cloth out to the back of their property at midnight that evening. Mike would dig a three-foot by three-foot hole while Amber held a flashlight and supervised his digging. They were then to bury the dishcloth and to sit without speaking in the dark for ten minutes. During that time period, they were to think about the meaning of the task I had given them (I said that I would not give them any indication of what the true meaning of the task was). When they were done with the task, they were to go to bed without speaking until the next morning.

Amber and Mike were shocked by their assignment, but I was very surprised at how quickly they agreed to it. I believe that Mike agreed because there was no mention about his drinking and it brought Amber back home. Amber said she had a feeling that they needed something radical to help change their lives and she willing to do anything that might help. I commended them for their dedication to the assignment and to their relationship. When asked why I gave them this specific task, I again stated that knowing the meaning was not part of the assignment. I quickly ended the session and sent them home.

I did not see Amber and Mike for three weeks, however, when they came in for their session, they immediately told me of how transformational their ritual assignment had been for them. They detailed how difficult it was to deal with the smell of the dishcloth sitting on the counter for three straight days. They also described how difficult it was for Mike to dig a three-foot by three-foot hole in the dark. Amber had held a flashlight for him and measured the hole to see if it was the required depth. Something surprising happened toward the end of their ritual task, when Mike suddenly told Amber that he had an idea and ran back into the house. Mike returned with an empty beer bottle, which he threw into the hole with the dishcloth. After they had buried the dishcloth and the beer bottle, they both sat quietly for the required amount of time and then went to bed.

Mike was quick to let me know how tough it was to dig a three-foot by three-foot hole in the dark. He had even thought about quitting, but he said Amber had continued to encourage him to finish the task.

Amber told me that standing and holding the flashlight for Mike was an odd experience because, even though she was trying to help him, she felt that standing over him was not comfortable for her. She said that she wanted to get a shovel and to help him dig, but she reminded herself that he was the one that was supposed to dig the hole.

After telling me about their experiences with the task, Amber and Mike then told me about the changes that had taken place. Mike said that he had begun controlling his drinking. He intentionally limited his beer consumption. He had begun setting a limit on how much he would drink every night and had not drunk to intoxication since burying the dishcloth and beer bottle. He admitted that he felt much more clear-headed with the children. He also said that the past three weeks had been wonderful since Amber was not only back home, but she seemed much happier. Amber agreed that she was happier. She also said that she had noticed that she had decreased some of her enabling behavior. She was also trying to focus more on the things which were good about their marriage, rather than what she didn't like.

My clients then asked me if I would tell them what the meaning of their task was. I told them that I was more interested in hearing what they believed it meant. Mike spoke up first and said that he realized that digging the hole and burying the cloth showed him that his marriage was dying. He said that he realized that if he continued his intoxicated behavior, he was burying his marriage. Amber told me that for her the meaning of the task was that the sour, smelly dishcloth that lay on the counter for three days stood for the issues they had wanted to ignore without dealing with them. She also said that her supervising Mike showed her that she was acting as his superior instead of his equal. She knew she had to meet him on the same level rather than trying to manage him. She believed the task also showed her that they could work together more effectively. I complimented them both on finding the meaning for the mysterious task they had undertaken. I did not ever tell them that I personally had no real knowledge of what anything in the ritual meant. I had just followed an idea that popped into my mind and had run with it!

From that point on, both Amber and Mike were fully involved in both their therapy and in the marriage. We continued to work on Mike's fears of abandonment and Amber's enabling patterns. We explored how their communication could be improved and how their time together could become more enjoyable. At the end of our therapy, they both believed that they were in a good place to continue a healthy and committed marriage. As we wrapped up our last session, I asked if they could tell me what had been of the most benefit to them while they were in therapy. Both immediately said the therapeutic ritual of burying the small cloth was what transformed them. I was touched when Mike, with a glaze of moisture in his eyes, thanked me for having him dig the hole because he knew that his marriage had been saved by the task.

Clients already have what is needed for them to create a desirable change in their lives. It may be that they just need an out of the ordinary experiential process for the change to occur. Even though these unconscious symbolic tasks are not stand-alone therapies, they can aid therapists who have reached the limits of what a conscious understanding can do. Rituals can connect us to parts of ourselves to which we have lost a connection. By having clients participate in a unique action, one not previously experienced, they gain more flexibility in how they relate to their problems. Rituals also give them an embodied sensation of being a part of something greater, which can help them in overcoming their perceived limitations. Rituals not only aid in interrupting habitual patterns, generating new experiences, and shifting client perceptions, they can also truly make a therapy session magical.

EPILOGUE

I think that it is important to recap the key elements for creating transformative sessions. Therapists create the conditions for transformational sessions when they are open to the unknown and allow themselves to work unhampered by standardized, rote ways of performing therapy. The best results come when attention is paid to building and maintaining a therapeutic relationship built on respect and feedback. Clients connect more deeply with therapists who are authentic, who possess a healing presence, and who actively encourage positive expectancy for change. Therapists who allow themselves the flexibility to follow their own intuition, freely improvise, and utilize any aspect of a session help to make therapy an alive and dynamic experience which helps in changing clients' brains and minds. Magic comes when we move away from the pathology laden themes of discourse and move toward empowering, resourceful themes. Viewing client problems and solutions from a nonlinear perspective encourages more creative sessions filled with new possibilities for clients. Designing and implementing new rituals also give clients out of the ordinary magical experiences and helps to break the spell of limiting patterns of interaction.

When all of these elements are present, therapy takes on a different feeling for both the therapist and the client. There is a new context of healing. There is more emphasis on connection and less focus on technique. There is more investigation of client strengths and less of client weaknesses. There is more focus on the present moment and less on preplanned actions. There is more openness toward potential and less on stagnation. There is more appreciation for spontaneity and less for regimentation. These key elements create a new and engaging manner of interaction that is both beautiful and mysterious. When we allow ourselves an entrance into this enchanted place, we make psychotherapy much more than just an empirical-based process for alleviating mental disorders, we make it magical.

REFERENCES

Ackerman, S.J., & Hilsenroth, M.J. (2003). A review of therapist characteristics and techniques positively impacting the therapeutic alliance. *Clinical Psychology Review*, 23(1), 1-33.

Adler, L.L., & Mukherji, B.R. (1995). *Spirit Versus Scalpel: Traditional Healing and Modern Psychotherapy*. Westport, CT: Bergin & Garvey.

Amble, I., Gude, T., Ulvenes, P., Stubdal, S., & Wampold, B.E. (2016). How and when feedback works in psychotherapy: Is it the signal?. *Psychotherapy Research*, 26(5), 545-555.

Armstrong, C. (2015). *The Therapeutic 'aha!': 10 Strategies for Getting Your Clients Unstuck*. New York, NY: WW Norton & Company.

Bateson, G. (1971). The cybernetics of 'self': A theory of alcoholism. *Psychiatry*, 34(1), 1-18.

Bateson, G. (1979). *Mind and Nature: A Necessary Unity*. New York, NY: Dutton.

Blow, A.J., Sprenkle, D.H., & Davis, S.D. (2007). Is who delivers the treatment more important than the treatment itself? The role of the therapist in common factors. *Journal of Marital and Family Therapy*, 33(3), 298-317.

Bohart, A.C. (1999). Intuition and creativity in psychotherapy. *Journal of Constructivist Psychology*, 12(4), 287-311.

Bohart, A.C., & Tallman, K. (1999). *How Clients Make Therapy Work: The Process of Active Self-healing*. Washington, DC: American Psychological Association.

Bohart, A.C., & Tallman, K. (2010). Clients: The neglected common factor in psychotherapy. In Duncan, B.L., Miller, S.D., Wampold, B.E., & Hubble, M.A. (Eds.). *The Heart and Soul of Change: Delivering What Works in Therapy*. (2nd Ed.) (pp. 83-112). Washington, DC: American Psychological Association.

Bradshaw, J. (2012). APA leading the charge against 'medicalizing' DSM-5. *The National Psychologist*, 21(1), 1-3.

Bugental, J.F.T. (1989). *The Search for Existential Identity*. San Francisco, CA: Josey-Bass.

Burns, T.R., & Engdahl, E. (1998). The social construction of consciousness. Part 2: Individual selves, self-awareness, and reflectivity. *Journal of Consciousness Studies*, 5(2), 166-184.

Cabane, O.F. (2013). *The Charisma Myth: How Anyone Can Master the Art and Science of Personal Magnetism*. New York, NY: Penguin.

Campbell, J., & Moyers, B. (1988). *The Power of Myth*. New York, NY: Anchor.

Cappas, N.M., Andres-Hyman, R., & Davidson, L. (2005). What psychotherapists can begin to learn from neuroscience: Seven principles of a brain-based psychotherapy. *Psychotherapy: Theory, Research, Practice, Training*, 42(3), 374.

Carson, D.K., & Becker, K.W. (2004). When lightning strikes: Reexamining creativity in psychotherapy. *Journal of Counseling & Development*, 82(1), 111–115.

Caspar, F., & Berger, T. (2012). Corrective experiences: What can we learn from different models and research in basic psychology? In Castonguay, L.G., & Hill, C.E. (Eds.). *Transformation in Psychotherapy: Corrective Experiences Across Cognitive Behavioral, Humanistic, and Psychodynamic Approaches*. (pp. 141–157). Washington, DC: American Psychological Association.

Castillo, R.J. (2001). Lessons from folk healing practices. In Tseng, W., & Streltzer, J. (Eds.). *Culture and Psychotherapy: A Guide to Clinical Practice*. (pp. 81–101). Washington, DC: American Psychiatric Press.

Castonguay, L.G., & Hill, C.E. (2012). *Transformation in Psychotherapy: Corrective Experiences Across Cognitive Behavioral, Humanistic, and Psychodynamic Approaches*. Washington, DC: American Psychological Association.

Cheetham, R.W.S., & Griffiths, J.A. (1992). The traditional healer/diviner as psychotherapist. *South African Medical Journal*, 62(11), 957–958.

Chenail, R., Keeney, B., & Keeney, H. (2015). Recursive frame analysis: A qualitative research method for mapping change-oriented discourse. *The Qualitative Report*, 17(38), 1–15.

Cole, V.L. (2003). Healing principles: A model for the use of ritual in psychotherapy. *Counseling and Values*, 47(3), 184–194.

Constantino, M.J., Penek, S., Bernecker, S. L., & Overtree, C. E. (2014). A preliminary examination of participant characteristics in relation to patients' treatment beliefs in psychotherapy in a training clinic. *Journal of Psychotherapy Integration*, 24(3), 238.

Da Silva, J. (2008). *The effect of psychotherapist charisma on client satisfaction* (Doctoral dissertation, ProQuest Information & Learning).

Dolan, Y.M. (1985). *A Path with a Heart: Ericksonian Utilization with Resistant and Chronic Clients*. New York, NY: Brunner/Mazel.

Duncan, B. (2010). On becoming a better therapist. *Psychotherapy in Australia*, 16(4), 42.

Duncan, B.L., Miller, S.D., Wampold, B.E., & Hubble, M.A. (2010). *The Heart and Soul of Change: Delivering What Works in Therapy*. (2nd Ed.). Washington, DC: American Psychological Association.

Egnew, T.R. (2005). The meaning of healing: Transcending suffering. *Annals of Family Medicine*, 3(3), 255–262.

Elliott, R., & Greenberg, L. (2007). The essence of process-experiential: Emotion-focused therapy. *American Journal of Psychotherapy*, 61(3), 241–254.

Elkins, D. (2009). The medical model in psychotherapy: An explanatory system that fails to explain. *Journal of Humanistic Psychology*, 49(1), 267–291.

Farley, N. (2017). Improvisation as a meta-counseling skills. *Journal of Creativity in Mental Health*, 12(1), 115–128.

Feinstein, R., Heiman, N., & Yager, J. (2015). Common factors affecting psychotherapy outcomes: Some implications for teaching psychotherapy. *Journal of Psychiatric Practice*, 21, 180–189.

Finlay, L., & Gough, B. (Eds.). (2008). *Reflexivity: A Practical Guide for Researchers in Health and Social Sciences*. Oxford: Blackwell Science.

Flemons, D.G. (1991). *Completing Distinctions: Interweaving the Ideas of Gregory Bateson and Taoism Into a Unique Approach to Therapy*. Boulder, CO: Shambhala Publications.

Flückiger, C., & Grosse Holtforth, M. (2008). Focusing the therapist's attention on the patient's strengths: A preliminary study to foster a mechanism of change in outpatient psychotherapy. *Journal of Clinical Psychology*, 64(7), 876–890.

Frank, J.D., & Frank, J.B. (1993). *Persuasion and Healing: A Comparative Study of Psychotherapy* (3rd Edition). Baltimore, MD: Johns Hopkins University Press.

Fraser, J.S., & Solovey, A.D. (2007). *Second-Order Change in Psychotherapy: The Golden Thread that Unifies Effective Treatments*. Washington, DC: American Psychological Association.

Galvez, Z., & Crouch, B. (2017). Developing resilience with the Improviser's mindset: Getting people out of their stuck places. In Marks-Tarlow, T., Siegel, D.J., & Solomon, M. (Eds.). *Play and Creativity in Psychotherapy (Norton Series on Interpersonal Neurobiology)*. (pp. 309–337). WW Norton & Company.

Gassmann, D., & Grawe, K. (2006). General change mechanisms: The relation between problem activation and resource activation in successful and unsuccessful therapeutic interactions. *Clinical Psychology & Psychotherapy: An International Journal of Theory & Practice*, 13(1), 1–11.

Geller, S.M., & Greenberg, L.S. (2012). *Therapeutic Presence: A Mindful Approach to Effective Therapy*. Washington, DC: American Psychological Association.

Gergen, K. J. (2009). *Relational Being: Beyond Self and Community*. Oxford: Oxford University Press.

Gibney, P. (2012). Reimagining psychotherapy: An interview with Hillary and Bradford Keeney. *Psychotherapy in Australia*, 8(3), 62–71.

Goodwyn, E.D. (2016). *Healing Symbols in Psychotherapy: A Ritual Approach*. New York, NY: Routledge.

Goldfield, M.R. (2012). The corrective experience: A core principle for therapeutic change. In Castonguay, L.G., & Hill, C.E. (Eds.). *Transformation in Psychotherapy: Corrective Experiences Across Cognitive Behavioral, Humanistic, and Psychodynamic Approaches*. (pp. 13–29). Washington, DC: American Psychological Association.

Greenberg, L.S., & Paivio, S. C. (2003). *Working with Emotions in Psychotherapy* (Vol. 13). New York, NY: Guilford Press.

Greenberg, R.P. (2016). The rebirth of psychosocial importance in a drug filled world. *American Psychologist*, 71(8), 781–791.

Greenberg, R.P., Constantino, M. J., & Bruce, N. (2006). Are patient expectations still relevant for psychotherapy process and outcome? *Clinical Psychology Review*, 26(6), 657–678.

Haley, J. (1973). *Uncommon Therapy: The Psychiatric Techniques of Milton H. Erickson, M.D.* New York, NY: Norton.

Hansen, B., Howe, A., Sutton, P., & Ronan, K. (2015). Impact of client feedback on clinical outcomes for young people using public mental health services: A pilot study. *Psychiatry Research*, 229(1), 617–619.

Heide, F.J. (2013). 'Easy to sense but hard to define': Charismatic nonverbal communication and the psychotherapist. *Journal of Psychotherapy Integration*, 23(3), 305.

Hill, R., & Rossi, E. (2017). *The Practitioners' Guide to Mirroring Hands: Responsive Therapy that Unlocks Natural Problem Solving and Mind-Body Healing*. Carmarthen: Crown House Publishing Ltd.

Hinton, D.E., & Kirmayer, L.J. (2017). The flexibility hypothesis of healing. *Culture, Medicine, and Psychiatry*, 41(1), 3–34.

Hogue, D.A. (2006). Healing of the self-in-context: Memory, plasticity, and spiritual practice. In Koss-Chioino, J., & Hefner, P.J. (Eds.). *Spiritual Transformation and Healing: Anthropological, Theological, Neuroscientific, and Clinical Perspectives*. (pp. 223–38). AltaMira Press, MD: Lanham.

Holtforth, M.G., Krieger, T., Bochsler, K., & Mauler, B. (2011). The prediction of psychotherapy success by outcome expectations in inpatient psychotherapy. *Psychotherapy and Psychosomatics*, 80(5), 321–322.

Horowitz, R. (2008). Hope and expectation in the psychotherapy of the long-term mentally ill. *Bulletin of the Menninger Clinic*, 72(4), 237–258.

Horvath, A.O., & Bedi, R.P. (2002). The alliance. In Norcross, C. (Ed.). *Psychotherapy Relationships That Work: Therapist Contributions and Responsiveness to Patients*. (pp. 37–69). Oxford: Oxford University Press.

Imber-Black, E. (2003). Ritual themes in families and family therapy. In Imber-Black, E., Roberts, J., & Whiting, R.A. (Eds.). (2003). *Rituals in Families and Family Therapy* (pp. 49–87). New York, NY: WW Norton & Company.

Jeffrey, A.J., & Stone Fish, L. (2011). Clinical intuition: A qualitative study of its use and experience among marriage and family therapists. *Contemporary Family Therapy*, 33(4), 348–363.

Jodorowsky, A. (2015). *Manual of Psychomagic: The Practice of Shamanic Psychotherapy*. Rochester, VT: Inner Traditions.

Johnson, S.M. (2002). *Emotionally Focused Couple Therapy with Trauma Survivors: Strengthening Attachment Bonds*. New York, NY: Guilford Press.

Johansen, R., Iversen, V.C., Melle, I., & Hestad, K.A. (2013). Therapeutic alliance in early schizophrenia spectrum disorders: A cross-sectional study. *Annals of General Psychiatry*, 12(1), 14.

Johanson, G., & Kurtz, R. (1991). *Grace Unfolding: Psychotherapy in the Spirit of Tao Te Ching*. New York, NY: Bell Tower Books.

Jonas, W.B., & Crawford, C.C. (2004). The healing presence: Can it be reliably measured?. *Journal of Alternative & Complementary Medicine*, 10(5), 751–756.

Joyce, A.S., Piper, W.E., & Ogrodniczuk, J.S. (2007). Therapeutic alliance and cohesion variables as predictors of outcome in short-term group psychotherapy. *International Journal of Group Psychotherapy*, 57(3), 269–296.

Keeney, B.P. (1983). *Aesthetics of Change*. New York, NY: Guilford.

Keeney, B. (2009). *The Creative Therapist: The Art of Awakening a Session*. New York, NY: Routledge.

Keeney, H., & Keeney, B. (2013a). *Creative Therapeutic Technique: Skills for the Art of Bringing Forth Change*. Zeig, Tucker & Theisen.

Keeney, B., & Keeney, H. (2013b). Reentry into first creation: A contextual frame for the Ju/'hoan Bushman performance of puberty rites, storytelling, and healing dance. *Journal of Anthropological Research*, 69(1), 65–86.

Kershaw, C., & Wade, J.W. (2011). *Brain Change Therapy: Clinical Interventions for Self-Transformation*. New York, NY: WW Norton & Company.

Kindler, R.C., & Gray, A.A. (2010). Theater and therapy: How improvisation informs the analytic hour. *Psychoanalytic Inquiry*, 30(3), 254–266.

146

Kirmayer, L.J. (1999). Myth and ritual in psychotherapy. *Transcultural Psychiatry*, 36(4), 451–460.

Kottler, J.A., & Carlson, J. (2009). *Creative Breakthroughs in Therapy: Tales of Transformation and Astonishment*. Hoboken, NJ: Wiley.

Knoblauch, S.H. (2001). High-risk, high-gain choices: Commentary on paper by Philip A. Ringstrom. *Psychoanalytic Dialogues*, 11(5), 785–795.

Krippner, S. (2012). Shamans as healers, counselors, and psychotherapists. *International Journal of Transpersonal Studies*, 31(2), 9.

Laderman, C., & Roseman, M. (1996). *The Performance of Healing*. New York, NY: Routledge.

Lambert, M.J., & Shimokawa, K. (2011). Collecting client feedback. *Psychotherapy*, 48(1), 72.

Laquercia, T. (2005). Listening with the intuitive ear. *Modern Psychoanalysis*, 30(1), 60–72.

Laska, K.M., Gunman, A.S., & Wampold, B.E. (2014). Expanding the lens of evidence-based practice in psychotherapy: A common factors perspective. *Psychotherapy*, 51(4), 467–481.

Laub, L. (2006). Intuitive listening. *Modern Psychoanalysis*, 31(1), 88–101.

Lawrence, C., Foster, V.A., & Tieso, C.L. (2015). Creating creative clinicians: Incorporating creativity into counselor education. *Journal of Creativity in Mental Health*, 10, 166–180.

Leary, M.R., & Tangney, J.P. (2003). The self as an organizing construct in the behavioral and social sciences. *Handbook of Self and Identity*. New York, NY: Guilford Press.

LeDoux, J. (1998). *The Emotional Brain: The Mysterious Underpinnings of Emotional Life*. New York, NY: Simon and Schuster.

LeShan, L.L. (1996). *Beyond Technique: Psychotherapy for the 21st Century*. Northvale, NJ: Jason Aronson.

Lutz, W., De Jong, K., & Rubel, J. (2015). Patient-focused and feedback research in psychotherapy: Where are we and where do we want to go?. *Psychotherapy Research*, 25(6), 625–632.

Magical [Def. 2]. (2018). English Oxford Living Dictionary Online. Retrieved April 9, 2018, from https://en.oxforddictionaries.com/definition/magical

Marks-Tarlow, T. (2012). *Clinical Intuition in Psychotherapy: The Neurobiology of Embodied Response*. New York, NY: WW Norton & Company.

Marks-Tarlow, T. (2014a). The nonlinear dynamics of clinical intuition. *Chaos and Complexity Letters*, 8(2/3), 147.

Marks-Tarlow, T. (2014b). Clinical intuition at play. *American Journal of Play*, 6(3), 392.

Maturana H.R. (1988). Reality: The search for objectivity or the quest for a compelling argument. *Irish Journal of Psychology*, 9(1), 25–82.

Maturana, H.R., & Varela, F.J. (1987). *The Tree of Knowledge: The Biological Roots of Human Understanding*. Boulder, CO: Shambhala Publications.

McCabe, G. (2008). Mind, body, emotions and spirit: Reaching to the ancestors for healing. *Counselling Psychology Quarterly*, 21(2), 143–152.

McDonough-Means, S.I., Kreitzer, M.J., & Bell, I.R. (2004). Fostering a healing presence and investigating its mediators. *Journal of Alternative & Complementary Medicine*, 10(Supplement 1), S-25–S-41.

McNeilly, R. (2014). *Creating Connections, Volume One: Selected Papers of Rob McNeilly*. Newcastle, Australia: Tandava Press.

Miller, S.D., & Hubble, M. (2017). How psychotherapy lost its magick: The art of healing in an age of science. *Psychotherapy Networker*, 41(2), 26–37.

Miller, S.D., Duncan, B., & Hubble, M. (2008). Supershrinks: What is the secret of their success?. *Psychotherapy in Australia*, 14(4), 14.

Miller, S.D., Hubble, M.A., Chow, D., & Seidel, J. (2015). Beyond measures and monitoring: Realizing the potential of feedback-informed treatment. *Psychotherapy*, 52(4), 449.

Mitchell, C.W. (2012). *Effective Techniques for Dealing with Highly Resistant Clients.* (2nd Ed.). Johnson City, TN: Clifton Mitchell Publications.

Montuori, A. (2003). The complexity of improvisation and the improvisation of complexity: Social science, art and creativity. *Human Relations*, 56(2), 237–255.

Moodley, R., Sutherland, P., & Oulanova, O. (2008). Traditional healing, the body and mind in psychotherapy. *Counselling Psychology Quarterly*, 21(2), 153–165.

Moore, R.L. (1983). Contemporary psychotherapy as ritual process: An initial reconnaissance. *Zygon*, 18(3), 283–293.

Mozdzierz, G.J., Peluso, P.R., & Lisiecki, J. (2014). *Advanced Principles of Counseling and Psychotherapy: Learning, Integrating, and Consolidating the Nonlinear Thinking of Master Practitioners.* New York, NY: Routledge.

Nardone, G. (1996). *Brief Strategic Solution-Oriented Therapy of Phobic and Obsessive Disorders.* Northvale, NJ: Jason Aronson.

Nardone, G., & Balbi, E. (2008). *The Logic of Therapeutic Change: Fitting Strategies to Pathologies.* London: Karnac.

Neill, J.R., & Kniskern, D. P. (Eds.). (1982). *From Psyche to System: The Evolving Therapy of Carl Whitaker.* New York, NY: Guilford Press.

Norcross, J.C. (2010). The therapeutic relationship. In Duncan, B.L., Miller, S.D., Wampold, B.E., & Hubble, M.A. (Eds.). *The Heart and Soul of Change: Delivering What Works in Therapy* (pp. 113–141). Washington, DC: American Psychological Association.

Norcross, J.C., & Wampold, B.E. (2011). What works for whom: Tailoring psychotherapy to the person. *Journal of Clinical Psychology*, 67(2), 127–132.

O'Hanlon, W.H. (1987). *Taproots: Underlying Principles of Milton Erickson's Therapy and Hypnosis.* New York, NY: Norton.

Okiishi, J.C., Lambert, M.J., Eggett, D., Nielsen, L., Dayton, D.D., & Vermeersch, D.A. (2006). An analysis of therapist treatment effects: Toward providing feedback to individual therapists on their clients' psychotherapy outcome. *Journal of Clinical Psychology*, 62(9), 1157–1172.

Okiishi, J., Lambert, M.J., Nielsen, S.L., & Ogles, B.M. (2003). Waiting for supershrink: An empirical analysis of therapist effects. *Clinical Psychology & Psychotherapy*, 10(6), 361–373.

Orlinsky, D.E., & Rønnestad, M.H. (2005). *How Psychotherapists Develop: A Study of Therapeutic Work and Professional Growth.* Washington, DC: American Psychological Association.

Orlinsky, D.E., Rønnestad, M.H., & Willutzki, U. (2004). Fifty years of psychotherapy process-outcome research: Continuity and change. In Lambert, M.J. (Ed.). *Bergin and Garfield's Handbook of Psychotherapy and Behavior Change.* (pp. 307–389). New York, NY: Wiley.

Pagano, C.J. (2012). Exploring the therapist's use of self: Enactments, improvisation and affect in psychodynamic psychotherapy. *American Journal of Psychotherapy*, 66(3), 205-226.

Patterson, C.L., Anderson, T., & Wei, C. (2014). Clients' pretreatment role expectations, the therapeutic alliance, and clinical outcomes in outpatient therapy. *Journal of Clinical Psychology*, 70(7), 673-680.

Priebe, S., Richardson, M., Cooney, M., Adedeji, O., & McCabe, R. (2011). Does the therapeutic relationship predict outcomes of psychiatric treatment in patients with psychosis? A systematic review. *Psychotherapy and Psychosomatics*, 80(2), 70-77.

Ringstrom, P.A. (2003). 'Crunches,' '(k)nots,' and double binds—When what isn't happening is the most important thing: Commentary on paper by Barbara Pizer. *Psychoanalytic Dialogues*, 13(2), 193-205.

Ringstrom, P.A. (2008). Improvisation and mutual inductive identification in couples therapy: Commentary on paper by Susan M. Shimmerlik. *Psychoanalytic Dialogues*, 18(3), 390-402.

Ringstrom, P.A. (2011). Principles of improvisation: A model of therapeutic play in relational psychoanalysis. In Aron, L., & Harris, A. (Eds.). *Relational Psychoanalysis*. (pp. 447-474). Hillsdale, NJ: The Analytic Press.

Romanelli, A., Tishby, O., & Moran, G.S. (2017). 'Coming home to myself': A qualitative analysis of therapists' experience and interventions following training in theater improvisation skills. *The Arts in Psychotherapy*, 53, 12-22.

Ross, J., & Werbart, A. (2013). Therapist and relationship factors influencing dropout from individual psychotherapy: A literature review. *Psychotherapy Research*, 23, 394-418.

Rossi, E.L. (2001). The deep psychobiology of psychotherapy. In Corsini, R. (Ed.). *Handbook of Innovative Therapy*. (2nd Ed.) (pp. 155-165). New York, NY. Wiley.

Rossi, E.L. (2002). *The Psychobiology of Gene Expression: Neuroscience and Neurogenesis in Hypnosis and the Healing Arts*. New York, NY: WW Norton & Company.

Rouse, A., Armstrong, J., & McLeod, J. (2015). Enabling connections: Counsellor creativity and therapeutic practice. *Counselling and Psychotherapy Research*, 15(3), 171-179.

Rutherford, B.R., Wager, T.D., & Roose, S.P. (2010). Expectancy and the treatment of depression: a review of experimental methodology and effects on patient outcome. *Current Psychiatry Reviews*, 6(1), 1-10.

Schiepek, G., Eckert, H., Aas, B., Wallot, S., & Wallot, A. (2015). *Integrative Psychotherapy: A Feedback-driven Dynamic Systems Approach*. Boston, MA: Hogrefe Publishing.

Schneider, K. (2015). Presence: The core contextual factor of effective psychotherapy. *Existential Analysis: Journal of the Society for Existential Analysis*, 26(2), 304-312.

Schnellbacher, J., & Leijssen, M. (2009). The significance of therapist genuineness from the client's perspective. *Journal of Humanistic Psychology*, 49(2), 207-228.

Schore, A. N. (2012). *The Science of the Art of Psychotherapy (Norton Series on Interpersonal Neurobiology)*. New York, NY: WW Norton & Company.

Siegel, D.J. (1999). *The Developing Mind: Toward a Neurobiology of Interpersonal Experience*. New York, NY: Guilford Press.

Siegel, D.J. (2010). *The Mindful Therapist: A Clinician's Guide to Mindsight and Neural Integration*. New York, NY: WW Norton & Company.

Slone, N.C., Reese, R.J., Mathews-Duvall, S., & Kodet, J. (2015). Evaluating the efficacy of client feedback in group psychotherapy. *Group Dynamics: Theory, Research, and Practice*, 19(2), 122.

Spolin, V. (1999). *Improvisation for the Theater: A Handbook of Teaching and Directing Techniques*. (3rd Ed.). Evanston, IL: Northwestern University Press.

Strupp, H.H., & Hadley, S.W. (1979). Specific vs nonspecific factors in psychotherapy: A controlled study of outcome. *Archives of General Psychiatry*, 36(10), 1125-1136.

Tantia, J.F. (2014). Is intuition embodied? A phenomenological study of clinical intuition in somatic psychotherapy practice. *Body, Movement and Dance in Psychotherapy*, 9(4), 211-223.

Torrey, E.F. (1986). *Witchdoctors and Psychiatrists: The Common Roots of Psychotherapy and its Future*. San Francisco, CA: HarperCollins.

Tracey, T.J., Wampold, B.E., Lichtenberg, J.W., & Goodyear, R.K. (2014). Expertise in psychotherapy: An elusive goal? *American Psychologist*, 69(3), 218.

Usandivaras, R. (1985). The therapeutic process as a ritual. *Group Analysis*, 18(1), 8-16.

Van der Hart, O. (1983). *Rituals in Psychotherapy: Transition and Continuity*. New York, NY: Ardent Media.

Varela, F. (1979). *Principles of Biological Autonomy*. New York, NY: North Holland.

Voutilainen, L., Peräkylä, A., & Ruusuvuori, J. (2010). Recognition and interpretation: Responding to emotional experience in psychotherapy. *Research on Language and Social Interaction*, 43(1), 85-107.

Wampold, B.E. (2006). The psychotherapist. In Norcross, J.C., Beutler, L.E., & Levant, R. F. (Eds.). *Evidence-Based Practices in Mental Health: Debate and Dialogue on the Fundamental Questions* (pp. 200-208). Washington, DC: American Psychological Association.

Wampold, B.E. (2015). How important are the common factors in psychotherapy? An update. *World Psychiatry*, 14(3), 270-277.

Wampold, B.E., & Brown, G.S.J. (2005). Estimating variability in outcomes attributable to therapists: A naturalistic study of outcomes in managed care. *Journal of Consulting and Clinical Psychology*, 73(5), 914.

Watzlawick, P., Weakland, J.H., & Fisch, R. (1974). *Change: Principles of Problem Formation and Problem Resolution*. New York, NY: Norton.

Weis, M.L. (2009). A phenomenological investigation of licensed professional counselors' perspectives of clinical intuition (Doctoral dissertation, The University of North Carolina at Charlotte).

Welling, H. (2005). The intuitive process: The case of psychotherapy. *Journal of Psychotherapy Integration*, 15(1), 19-47.

Westra, H.A., Constantino, M.J., & Aviram, A. (2011). The impact of alliance ruptures on client outcome expectations in cognitive behavioral therapy. *Psychotherapy Research*, 21(4), 472-481.

Winek, J.L., & Craven, P.A. (2003). Healing rituals for couples recovering from adultery. *Contemporary Family Therapy*, 25(3), 249-266.

Wyrostock, N. (1995). The ritual as psychotherapeutic intervention. *Psychotherapy*, 32(3), 397-404.

Yalom, I. (2002). *The Gift of Therapy: Reflections on Being a Therapist.* London: Piatkus.

Yeh, C.J., Hunter, C.D., Madan-Bahel, A., Chiang, L., & Arora, A.K. (2004). Indigenous and interdependent perspectives of healing: Implications for counseling and research. *Journal of Counseling & Development,* 82(4), 410–419.

Zeig, J.K. (Ed.). (1994). *Ericksonian Methods: The Essence of the Story.* London: Routledge.

INDEX